BANANA COOKBOOK

Reba E. Shepard

First published 1986 by
MACMILLAN EDUCATION LTD
London and Oxford
Companies and representatives throughout the world

www.macmillan-caribbean.com

ISBN 0–333–40961–2

18 17 16 15 14 13 12 11 10   9
10 09 08 07 06 05 04 03 02 01

This book is printed on paper suitable for recycling and
made from fully managed and sustained forest sources.

Printed in Malaysia

A catalogue record for this book is available from the
British Library.

Cover and chapter heading illustrations by George Craig

CONTENTS

Dedication

To the two people in my life
who stuck with me
through
five stalks of bananas —
my loving husband, Larry,
and
my devoted son, Michael.
Weaker men might have rebelled.

PREFACE

Legend has it in certain areas of the world that the forbidden fruit of the Garden of Eden was the banana, not the apple; that Adam and Eve used banana leaves to cover their nudity. Whatever the truth may be, the botanical name of the banana, *Musa sapientum*, means 'fruit of the wise' and certainly for hundreds of years, it has been a highly valued food source.

Authorities generally agree that the wild banana originated in the islands of Indonesia and slowly found its way to India, Africa and Arabia. As in the case of most wild fruit (actually the banana is not a fruit, but a herb), wild bananas were unappetising and full of seeds. It took centuries of cultivation and cross breeding to develop the flavourful and seedless banana of today. In the process, it was made sterile, unable to reproduce without human help. Bananas were introduced into the New World by the Spanish in the early 1500s, and they quickly adapted to the favourable climatic conditions of the Caribbean islands and to both Central and South America.

Plentiful and prolific, the banana has been a staple food in the tropics for hundreds of years, but being perishable and difficult to transport, it did not come into widespread use in North America and Europe until after World War I and the development of refrigeration and specifically designed banana boats. Today, this ancient herb has become a delightful addition to the daily diet of millions, and the discarded slippery banana peel has become a classic of Western cartoon humour.

I can truthfully say that it is the perishable nature of the banana that caused this book to be written. While cruising on our 47-foot sailing ketch, *Borne Free*, with my husband Larry and son Michael, we arrived at an anchorage close to the large island of Halmahera in north-eastern Indonesia. We were immediately surrounded by the inhabitants of the nearby small village in their primitive outrigger canoes, wanting to 'trade'. This had become a familiar sight to us in these out-of-the-way islands, where the local people rarely, if ever, see a foreign boat or yacht. We carried — for trading purposes — old clothing, knick-knacks and sugar. It was late, and we were tired, so we begged off until the next day. At dawn, we were awakened by muffled voices, clucking chickens and canoes banging against each other. A check of the clock showed it was 5.30 a.m. and the customers had arrived. We hauled ourselves out of bed, made a cup of instant coffee and put our gear out on deck.

After completing a very active trading session, we made friends of these people and the next day, as we prepared to depart, they generously gave us a gift of one of the few things that were plentiful in their primitive economy — five stalks of bananas, each stalk having 50 to 100 green bananas attached. We thanked them for their kindness, tied the stalks to the main boom to allow them to ripen and went on our way south through the Indonesian islands. Ripen they did — and predictably all at the same time! After a few days of a steady diet of bananas, I had run out of ideas for preparing them. My son Mike said: 'Mom, you have just got to figure out more ways to use bananas, and I've got the name of your third cookbook: *101 Ways to Use Bananas*.' At this point, as we travelled through the tropics, we all began to collect and test banana recipes. They have now been brought together in the book you hold in your hand.

There are well over a hundred varieties of bananas in the world today, but outside the area of the tropics only two varieties are widely distributed. First, there is the smooth-skinned, yellow banana, so familiar to us all, frequently called the 'dessert' banana. Hereafter in this book, we call it the *banana* in all recipes calling for its use. In contrast, the plantain is larger than the dessert banana and has a heavier and coarser skin. It is often seen in the market, still green and, in some cases, it is cooked while green. In this state, it has the consistency of raw potato or turnip and, indeed, it is frequently the staple form of starch in many tropical areas. As it slowly ripens, its use changes, but, unlike the dessert banana, it is never eaten raw, always cooked, even when fully ripe. It will be identified as *plantain* where used in this book. The dessert banana, raw or cooked, is both delicious and nutritious. Rich in carbohydrates, it also contains phosphorus, potassium and vitamins A and C. Some believe that a diet of bananas imparts wisdom, since the banana contains phosphorus, 'the salt of intelligence'. True or not, the banana is one of those foods that is not only good, it is good for you. Read on, taste and enjoy.

RECIPES

BREAKFASTS

The use of asterisks in this book indicates recipes mentioned elsewhere in the text.

BANANA BREAKFAST SHAKE

Combine in a blender	1 cup milk
	1 banana
	1 tsp vanilla
	1 egg
Optionally, add	$\frac{1}{4}$ cup wheatgerm
	pinch of cinnamon
	$\frac{1}{2}$ tsp honey or sugar
	4 Graham Crackers

Blend until smooth.
See also Fruit Cup* for another delicious breakfast drink.

BANANA OMELETTE

Sauté until soft	2 sliced bananas
in	3 tbs butter
Add	$\frac{1}{2}$ cup banana liqueur, or rum
mixed with	$\frac{1}{2}$ cup water
	1 tbs cornflour

Beat in another bowl   4 eggs
Mix with   3 tbs cream, or condensed milk
                            1 tbs sugar
                            1 tsp vanilla

Turn batter into heated, buttered pan. When set, add half of the banana sauce. Fold. Sprinkle with sugar and add remaining sauce. Serve immediately.

BANANAS IN BLANKETS

Equally good for breakfast, or as a side dish for meat, especially pork or chicken.

Cut into half lengthwise   1 banana per person
Between halves, place   canned-pineapple stick
Wrap around bananas   bacon slices

Secure with toothpicks. Grill in a pan, turning frequently until bacon is crisp.
See also Bananas 'n Bacon* and Baked Bananas in Bacon*.

BANANA FRENCH TOAST

Cut   slices of favourite bread
Mash in cup   2 medium, ripe bananas
Beat   2 eggs
with   2 tbs milk

Stir mashed bananas into egg mixture. Dip bread slices into the mixture, turning to make sure all of the bread is coated.
Heat in skillet   2 tbs vegetable oil
Add coated bread slices. Fry on one side until golden-brown, keeping heat low so that bread cooks and coating does not burn. Turn and fry other side.
Serve hot with butter and cinnamon sugar.

BANANA ENGLISH MUFFINS

Split and toast an English muffin. Butter it. Then spread each half with home-made Banana Jam*. Top with thinly sliced banana.
A quick, easy, excellent and nutritious breakfast.

HEAVENLY TRIPLE BANANA BREAKFAST MUFFINS

Mix together	1 pkg white cake mix (regular)
	1 pkg banana-flavoured instant pudding
	$\frac{1}{2}$ cup chopped walnuts
Separately, mix together	3 egg yolks
	$\frac{1}{2}$ cup mashed banana (overripe is fine)
	$\frac{1}{2}$ cup oil
	$\frac{1}{3}$ cup cream sherry

Stir liquid ingredients into dry. Then, either mix by hand until well blended and all ingredients are moistened and batter is smooth (about 3 minutes), or mix with electric mixer on medium speed (about 2 minutes).

Meanwhile, beat	3 egg whites
When they begin to stand, add	1 cup coarsely chopped or sliced, ripe banana

Continue to beat with electric mixer. Bananas will become puréed with beating. Beat until this mixture stands in peaks.

Carefully fold in by hand	$\frac{1}{2}$ cup banana, chopped or cut into $\frac{1}{4}$-inch cubes

Next, carefully fold this egg white/banana mixture into muffin batter mixture, until all trace of egg white is incorporated. Choose non-stick muffin tins, or spray tins with non-stick coating. Fill muffin cups to within $\frac{1}{2}$ inch of top. Place in preheated oven (350°F), on top rack, which has been placed about $\frac{1}{3}$ of the way from the top of the oven. Bake for 20 minutes. Do not check, or open oven door until 20 minutes are up. Then, remove from oven and insert toothpick in one muffin to test. (If toothpick comes out clean, muffins are cooked through.) Muffins should also be brown on top. Cool in pan for 5 minutes. Then invert pan and allow muffins to cool on wire rack.

FRUIT ROLL

Prepare Perfect Crusty Biscuit dough:

Combine	2 cups sifted flour
	$2\frac{1}{2}$ tsp baking powder
	1 tsp salt
With 2 knives, cut in	$\frac{1}{3}$ cup shortening

Work until mixture forms fine particles.

Add	up to $\frac{2}{3}$ cup milk (until dough holds together)

Gather dough into a ball, turn it on to a lightly floured board and knead gently with floured fingers. Roll biscuit dough into a $\frac{1}{4}$-inch thick rectangle.

Spread surface with	2 tbs butter
Scatter over it	2 cups diced banana
Sprinkle with	$\frac{1}{2}$ cup sugar
	$\frac{1}{2}$ tsp nutmeg
	1 tsp lemon juice

Roll over lengthwise like a jelly roll and place seam side down on a baking sheet, or pan, rubbed with butter. Seal ends of roll to prevent juice from running out, and bake at 400°F for 30 minutes. Serves 6.

BANANA COFFEE CAKE

Blend	2 tbs sugar
	1 egg
	1 cup mashed ripe banana
	2 cups biscuit mix

Beat well. Spread into greased 8×8×2 inch pan.

Blend	2 tsp cinnamon
	$\frac{1}{4}$ cup sugar
	2 tbs biscuit mix
	2 tbs butter

When crumbly, spread on cake batter. Top with nuts if desired. Bake at 400°F for 20–22 minutes, or until done when tested with a toothpick.

Alternatively, top with crushed cinnamon Graham Crackers.

BANANA CRUMB COFFEE CAKE

Dissolve	1 pkg yeast
in	$\frac{1}{4}$ cup warm water
Cream	$\frac{1}{2}$ cup butter
with	$\frac{1}{2}$ cup sugar
	$\frac{1}{8}$ tsp salt
Add	3 eggs
	$\frac{1}{4}$ cup milk
and .	dissolved yeast
Gradually add	$2\frac{1}{4}$ cups flour

Beat well after each addition. Spread batter into well-greased 9×9×2 inch pan.

Place	2–3 sliced bananas on dough
Prepare crumb topping:	
Combine	$\frac{2}{3}$ cup sugar
	$\frac{1}{2}$ cup flour
	2 tsp cinnamon
	6 tbs margarine

Mix together until like crumbs. Sprinkle over bananas on top of batter. Cover with aluminium foil and let rise in a warm spot for about an hour or until doubled in size. Bake at 375°F for 35–40 minutes. Cool on wire rack.

BANANA COFFEE ROLL

Dissolve	1 cake fresh yeast or 1 pkg dry yeast
in	$\frac{1}{4}$ cup lukewarm water
Separately, combine	$\frac{1}{2}$ cup scalded milk
	$\frac{1}{4}$ cup oil
	$\frac{1}{4}$ cup sugar
Add	yeast mixture
Cool to lukewarm.	
Add	$\frac{1}{4}$ cup cold water
Blend in	1 lightly beaten egg
Add gradually	3 cups sifted flour

Mix well, then knead for about a dozen strokes on a floured board. When smooth, roll into 8×12 inch rectangle.

Meanwhile, combine	2 tbs sugar
	1 tbs flour
	1 tsp cinnamon
	$\frac{1}{2}$ cup honey
	$\frac{1}{4}$ cup orange juice

Spread half of this mixture over dough and spread remainder in a 13×9×2 inch pan.

Over mixture on dough, spread	1$\frac{1}{2}$ cups diced, medium-ripe bananas
Sprinkle on	2 tbs brown sugar
	a little cinnamon
Dot with	butter

Roll, jelly-roll fashion, from the long edge. Cut into one-inch slices. Place slices, cut side down, in prepared pan. Let rise to double. Bake at 400°F for 25–30 minutes. Cool for 5 minutes before removing from pan.

BANANA BOATS
(grilled or baked)

For 4 servings:
Peel and cut in half, *crosswise*	4 small bananas
Mix	2 cups baking mix
with	$\frac{1}{2}$ cup water

When a soft dough forms, divide dough into 8 equal parts. Pat one part of dough around each piece of banana with fingers floured with baking mix. Completely cover banana. At this point, bananas can be covered and refrigerated up to 24 hours.

When ready to cook, brush cooking grid with oil and grill banana boats 4 inches from heat, turning frequently, until brown (about 15 minutes).

Or, bake wrapped bananas at 450°F uncovered, on greased cookie sheet until golden-brown (10–12 minutes).

BANANA BEIGNETS

Cut into 1-inch thick *pieces*	3–4 bananas (slightly underripe)

Place in a bowl.

Sprinkle with	juice of $\frac{1}{2}$ lemon
	2 tbs sugar
Pour on	$\frac{1}{4}$ cup white rum

Cover and marinate 40–50 minutes.

In a bowl, combine	1 cup sifted flour
	2 tsp sugar
Add	$\frac{1}{3}$ cup warm beer

Just blend together, but do not overbeat. If too thick, add water until batter is the consistency of heavy cream.

Add	2 tbs melted butter

Let batter set (40–60 minutes).

Heat	vegetable oil (to reach a depth of 3 inches in skillet)
While oil heats, beat	2 egg whites

Gently fold them into the batter. Drain banana slices and dip them into the batter. Drop 4–6 at a time into the hot fat and fry until they are nicely browned. Drain beignets on paper towels and sprinkle with lots of confectioner's sugar. Serve immediately, plain or with Apricot Sauce on page 7.

APRICOT SAUCE
In a small saucepan,
combine   1 cup apricot preserves
                         2 tbs lemon juice
                         1 tsp grated lemon rind
                         $\frac{1}{4}$ cup apricot brandy
                         2 tbs confectioner's sugar
Heat the mixture until the preserves dissolve. Strain through a sieve.
Then add $\frac{1}{4}$ cup kirsch
Chill the sauce and use for dunking Banana Beignets.

BANANA FRITTERS (1)
(easy)

Mash   1 lb ripe bananas
Add $\frac{3}{4}$ cup flour
                         1 tsp baking powder
                         $\frac{1}{4}$ cup sugar
                         $\frac{1}{2}$ tsp nutmeg
Mix well. Drop spoonfuls into hot oil. Fry until brown. Drain and
serve.

BANANA FRITTERS (2)
(more elegant)

Sift $1\frac{1}{4}$ cups flour
with   2 tsp baking powder
                         $\frac{1}{4}$ cup sugar
Separately, combine   1 well-beaten egg
                         6 tbs milk
                         2 tsp oil
Now, beat all together to make a batter.
Peel   2 ripe bananas
Cut into 3–4 pieces.
Roll in $\frac{1}{4}$ cup flour
Dip in   batter
Fry in hot (375°F) fat, turning to brown all sides. Drain on rack. Serve
plain, or add crisp bacon for a breakfast. (Dust with powdered sugar,
or serve with a hot fruit sauce as a pudding.) Serves 4.
See also Candied Banana Fritters*.

PANCAKES

For basic pancake recipe:

Combine	2 cups biscuit mix
	1 egg
	$1\frac{2}{3}$ cups milk

Beat ingredients together with rotary beater until smooth. Grease griddle. Turn pancakes when bubbles appear and before they break. Makes about 18 four-inch pancakes.

For thinner pancakes: add more milk. For thicker pancakes: add more biscuit mix.

BANANA PANCAKES

Make	basic quantity pancake batter
Add	1 cup mashed bananas
	1 tbs lemon juice
	2 tbs sugar

Cook as for pancakes. Serve with honey or currant jelly.

PUFF PANCAKES

To acquire even more individuality in breakfast dishes, we tried combining ingredients in a different order. With pancakes or waffles, the cook mixes her dry ingredients with liquid and eggs, cooks the mixture, and serves it with butter, fruit or syrup. Remembering the method of mixing dough for popovers, we heated the butter and water, added the dry ingredients all at once, then beat in the eggs, baked the mixture and served it with fruit. The result was as follows.

Bring to a boil in a saucepan	$\frac{1}{2}$ cup water
	$\frac{1}{4}$ cup butter
Add	$\frac{1}{2}$ cup pancake mix

Stir until smooth, then remove from heat.

Stir in, beating thoroughly after each addition	2 eggs

Mixture should be very smooth. Pour into buttered 9-inch glass pie dish. Bake in preheated oven at 500°F for 15–20 minutes until golden-brown and puffy. Remove from oven and slide on to serving plate. Top with your favourite topping.

Unlike the traditional pancakes with syrup or jam, Puff Pancakes can be served with a variety of different toppings for a versatile treat.

STRAWBERRIES AND WHIPPED CREAM
Defrost   1 pkg frozen strawberries
Pour into centre of Puff Pancakes.
Top with   whipped cream
Or pass cream separately.

FRESH BANANA
Melt in pan   1 jar apple jelly (about 1 cup)
Stir in   2 sliced bananas
Pour the mixture into the centre of Puff Pancakes.

BANANA AND NUTS
Mash   2 ripe bananas
Add   2 tbs brown sugar
                                 $\frac{1}{2}$ cup orange juice
Heat, then stir in $\frac{1}{4}$ cup chopped walnuts
Serve over Puff Pancakes.

BANANA WAFFLES

Combine   2 cups biscuit mix
                                 1 egg
                                 $1\frac{2}{3}$ cups milk
                                 2 tbs melted shortening
Beat ingredients together with rotary beater until smooth. Bake.
Makes three $9\frac{1}{4}$-inch waffles. For crisper waffles: add more milk. For
softer waffles: add more biscuit mix.
For an especially elegant waffle, separate eggs. Beat yolks into batter.
Then, separately, beat whites until stiff, but not dry, and fold into
batter.
Add to batter   1 cup mashed, ripe banana
                                 1 tbs lemon juice
                                 2 tbs sugar
Cook. Serve with currant jelly or dust with confectioner's sugar.

WHOLEWHEAT PANCAKES

This is a nourishing treat in a totally different pancake. Again, we
combine the ingredients differently, this time by folding beaten egg
whites and/or banana purée into the pancake batter. The batter can
be cooked as a pancake, or as a waffle, making two delightfully
different treats.

Sift together	2 cups wholewheat flour
	3 tsp baking powder
	1 tsp salt
	1 tbs brown sugar (or use honey and add it to the milk or oil)
Beat together	2 cups milk
	$\frac{1}{2}$ cup oil
	3 egg yolks

Combine with the dry ingredients. Beat the egg whites until very stiff. Fold in. Cook on greased griddle or in frying pan, or bake as a waffle in waffle iron.

Alternatively, make the batter with fruit purée instead of the milk. Some jars of baby food, such as banana, apple or apricot, can be used. Add fruit chunks or raisins to the batter, or try using tahina, nuts, sesame seeds or sunflower seeds. Use some cornmeal, or rolled oats, or buckwheat flour instead of wholewheat flour. For waffles, reduce milk or other liquid to $1\frac{3}{4}$ cups.

BANANA WHOLEWHEAT PANCAKES

Mash 2 ripe bananas into a cup. Top up the cup with milk, then add one cup of milk so that bananas and milk together make up 2 cups. Substitute this for the 2 cups of milk in the recipe for Wholewheat Pancakes.

CARAMEL BANANA CRÊPES

Prepare crêpes:

Beat together	$\frac{3}{4}$ cup flour
	$1\frac{1}{2}$ tsp sugar
	$\frac{1}{4}$ tsp baking powder
	$\frac{1}{4}$ tsp salt
	1 cup milk
	1 tbs melted butter
	$\frac{1}{4}$ tsp vanilla

When smooth, set aside and lightly grease a 7-inch or 8-inch skillet. Heat until hot.

For each crêpe, pour 2 tbs batter into skillet. Rotate skillet until batter covers the bottom. Cook until golden-brown. Gently loosen edge with spatula, turn and cook other side until golden-brown.

Stack crêpes, placing paper towel between them. Keep crêpes covered to prevent them from drying out. Makes about 12 crêpes.

Prepare filling:
In a one-quart
saucepan, mix together $\frac{1}{2}$ cup brown sugar (packed)
                             $\frac{1}{4}$ cup whipping cream
                             $\frac{1}{4}$ cup light corn syrup
                             2 tbs butter
                             $\frac{1}{2}$ tsp vanilla
Heat to just boiling, stirring occasionally.
Slice diagonally into hot
sauce   2–3 firm bananas
Stir carefully until slices are well coated.
In a chilled mixing
bowl, beat until stiff $1\frac{1}{4}$ cups whipping cream
To assemble: place crêpe on a dessert plate. Spoon on top 3–4 banana
slices with a little warm sauce. Top with about 2 tbs whipped cream.
Roll up. Repeat with remaining crêpes. Spoon rest of warm sauce over
crêpes. Top with whipped cream. Sprinkle with pecan halves. Makes
6–8 crêpe servings.

MAIN DISHES

MEXICAN CHICKEN WITH BANANAS

Dredge	pieces of chicken (for 6 servings)
in	seasoned flour
In a casserole, heat	2 tbs butter
and	2 tbs oil

Brown chicken pieces in fat, then remove from casserole.

In fat remaining, cook	2 onions, chopped
	2 cloves garlic, chopped
When translucent, mix in	juice from 14-oz can of whole Italian tomatoes
	remaining seasoned flour

Pour into casserole.

Add	3 carrots, thinly sliced
	reserved Italian tomatoes
	$\frac{1}{2}$ tsp oregano
	$\frac{1}{2}$ tsp red pepper flakes (or to taste)
	$\frac{1}{2}$ tsp thyme

Stir and cook until hot through. Return chicken to casserole.

Pour on	1 cup chicken broth, boiling
	$\frac{1}{2}$ cup dry white wine
Add	12–18 pitted prunes

Cook 20 minutes.

| *Add* | 3 firm bananas, peeled, sliced lengthwise and halved |

Cook covered for another 15 minutes, or until chicken is tender.

BANANA-STUFFED CHICKEN

George Marshall, single-handed skipper of *Santa Cruz de la Tenerife*, shared his favourite banana-flavoured main dish with us in December, 1979. He has no recollection of the source of the recipe, and merely says he has cooked it as long as he can recall.

Stuffing for one whole chicken:

Mix together	1 chopped onion
	1 clove garlic, mashed
	1 whole lemon, mashed, crushed, and skin slit
	mashed bananas

Fill cavity with mixture. Secure opening. Slit skin every inch in both directions on legs and breasts. Alternate tiny slices of garlic and larger slices of ginger in slits. Fresh ginger is best, but use candied if there is no fresh ginger root available. The dish is good with garlic only, but a completely different flavour is obtained by using garlic and ginger. Rub bird with oil, then salt, then pepper. Roast in foil or covered dish in a slow oven (250–300°F), until meat is tender — 2–2½ hours for a 4-lb bird.

BANANA CURRY

In a medium skillet, melt	2 oz butter
Fry until soft	2 small onions, chopped
Add	1 apple, peeled and diced
	½ tsp salt
Run boiling water over	3 oz sultanas

Add to apple/onion mixture.

| *Sprinkle in* | 1½ oz flour |
| | 2 tsp curry powder |

Stir and cook 3–4 minutes. Remove from heat.

| *Gradually stir in* | ½ pint milk |
| | ¼ pint water |

Return to heat and stir until thick.

| *Add* | 4 bananas, peeled and chopped |

Cook gently about 7 minutes.

Add   4 hard-boiled eggs, quartered

Continue cooking until eggs are heated through. Serve with boiled white rice and chutney.

BAKED FISH AND GREEN PLANTAINS

Peel and halve   4 green plantains
Parboil with   2 large onions, quartered
and   1 clove garlic
Drain. Remove garlic.
Split   1 large whole fish, or several smaller
                            fish
Rub inside with   split fresh lime.
                            salt and pepper

Arrange on rack of roasting pan. Surround with plantains and onions. Dot all with butter (about 3 tbs). Bake in moderate oven until fish is tender, basting frequently.

PIÑON

Peel and slice lengthwise   3 medium-ripe plantains
Lightly fry in   2 tbs butter
Meanwhile, prepare
mixture of   1 lb ground beef
                            $\frac{1}{2}$ cup minced onion
                            1 cup fine breadcrumbs
                            2 eggs
                            1 tsp coarse pepper
                            1 tsp salt

Make a circle out of each plantain slice. Secure with toothpick. Fill each circle with about $\frac{1}{2}$ cup meat mixture. Mound in the centre. Set circles in a greased baking pan. Bake at 350°F for 30–35 minutes, or until meat mixture is done.

SIDE DISHES

SEYCHELLES BANAE AU COCO

Peel	6 ripe bananas
Put in pan and cover	
with	2 tsp salt
	$\frac{1}{4}$ lb sugar
Add	milk made from 2 coconuts

Cook for 1 hour in oven.

Note: to prepare coconut milk, grate ripe coconuts into a bowl. Cover with boiling water. Strain and squeeze out liquid, using cheesecloth. If you have less than 2 cups of milk, repeat process using more boiling water.

BANANAS 'N BACON

For each serving:

Chop	2 slices bacon

Fry until crisp. Remove bacon with slotted spoon.

Slice	1 ripe banana

Fry in bacon fat until lightly browned. Turn. Fry second side. Sprinkle on bacon. Serve hot as a side dish.

See also Bananas in Blankets*.

BAKED BANANAS IN BACON

Cook until transparent   4 slices bacon
Brush with lemon juice   4 small, firm bananas, peeled
Wrap bacon around bananas, securing with toothpick. Place in shallow baking dish. Bake at 375°F for 25 minutes, or until done, turning once. Yields 4 servings.

BAKED BANANAS IN THEIR SKINS

Rub the skin of   1 banana per person
with   1 tbs butter, bacon fat or oil
Lay bananas on baking sheet. Bake at 350°F for 45 minutes. Serve one to each guest, and don't tell them what they are! Make them guess.

BLACK BANANAS

This is an unusual side dish, and guests are often baffled about what they are being served, until you show them how to peel and eat the banana.

Preheat oven to 375°F, or allow charcoal on a barbecue to set until the coals are glowing hot. Bake bananas in their skins in the oven or over hot coals for 20 minutes, or until bananas are absolutely black and shiny. On a grill, turn after 10 minutes.
When ready to serve, place one banana on each plate. Then, carefully peel back skin, or cut it open down the middle, sprinkle with lemon juice and confectioner's sugar, if desired. You can also add butter, or a little salt. Make it to your liking, and like it, you will!

BOILED GREEN BANANA

Indonesian dishes often include a simple green banana (maybe two days away from full ripening) boiled and unadorned like an albino hot dog. It is good with fish stew, or corned pork, or Sloppy Joes, with a little sweetening in the filling.

FRIED OR SAUTÉD PLANTAINS

Slice lengthwise into 4
pieces   underripe plantains
Arrange in pan with   4 tbs melted butter
Fry on medium heat until brown. Turn and brown second side.

Serve plain or as an accompaniment for meat, eggs or fish.
Or, sprinkle on   1 tbs cinnamon
mixed with   2 tbs sugar
This gives a completely different flavour.

CURRIED PLANTAINS

Peel and quarter   4 ripe plantains (colour has changed
                              from green to pale-yellow with brown
                              flecks)
Roll in   1 cup flour
seasoned with   1 tbs curry powder
                          1 tsp salt
                          pinch of pepper
Dip into   2 well-beaten eggs
Then in   1½ cups breadcrumbs
Fry until golden-brown in deep fat. Drain. Serve with meat or fish as a
vegetable.

BANANA CABBAGE SAUTÉ

In a skillet, melt   2 tbs butter
Add   4 cups shredded cabbage
                          1 tbs vinegar
                          1 tbs chopped parsley
                          ¼ tsp salt
                          pinch of pepper
Cook over medium heat, stirring constantly until cabbage is wilted.
Add   2 firm bananas, sliced
                          1 tbs chopped parsley
Cook a minute just to heat bananas through.
To reduce cabbage cooking odours, add 1 fresh lemon, cut into 4
wedges.

CANDIED PLANTAINS

Preheat oven to 375°F. Cover and cook one plantain per person in
boiling water until tender. Pare and cut plantains lengthwise into
½-inch slices. Place in shallow baking dish which has been well
buttered.

Sprinkle with	$\frac{3}{4}$ cup brown sugar
	$\frac{1}{2}$ tsp grated lemon rind
	$1\frac{1}{2}$ tbs lemon juice
	$\frac{1}{8}$ tsp ginger
and, if desired,	salt and pepper

Dot with butter. Bake uncovered for about 20 minutes.

CARAMELISED PLANTAINS

In a skillet, melt	$\frac{1}{2}$ cup orange marmalade
Add	4 medium-ripe, boiled plantains, cut into slices

Cook the plantains carefully in the sauce until they are coated on all sides and glazed and brown.

BANANA GREEN-BEAN BAKE

Cut into $\frac{1}{4}$-inch cubes	2 medium-ripe bananas
Fry lightly in	1 tbs butter

In a greased baking dish layer half of the bananas.

Sprinkle on	$\frac{1}{2}$ cup grated white cheese (mozzarella, jack, or munster)
Then add	1 pkg frozen, French-style green beans
Top with	$\frac{1}{2}$ cup grated cheese
Add	remaining bananas

Bake at 375°F for 15–20 minutes, or until heated through.

MEXICAN FRIED BANANAS
(*Plantanos Fritos*)

Bananas are often served as a vegetable with the simple, roasted or broiled meats and fowl that Mexicans frequently eat.

For one serving:

Peel and cut in half lengthwise	1 firm, green-tipped banana
In a wide frying pan, melt	$1\frac{1}{2}$ tsp butter or margarine

Place banana, cut side down, in butter and cook over medium-low heat for about 10 minutes, or until lightly browned. Serve warm.

FRIED BANANAS AND ONIONS

An unusual dish, it is, however, a Philippine favourite, so don't knock it until you try it.

Slice diagonally	firm, ripe bananas
Peel and slice thinly	2 medium onions

Sauté onions in butter until transparent. Remove from pan. Fry banana slices, a few at a time, until brown. When all are fried, add onions. Mix together and serve as a side dish with pork or fish.

BANANA-STUFFED PAPAYA

Slice in half lengthwise Remove the seeds.	1 nearly ripe papaya
Mash	3 ripe bananas
Add	$\frac{1}{2}$ tsp cream of coconut
	$\frac{1}{3}$ tsp nutmeg
	1 tsp rum

Stuff each papaya-half with banana mash. Dot with butter. Bake in 400°F oven for about 15 minutes — less if papaya shows signs of collapsing.

STUFFED-PAPAYA FLAMBÉ

Fill a small bowl with rum or brandy. Light and spoon the flaming liquor on to the fruit.

BANANA IGLOO

Chill the stuffed fruit as soon as you take it from the oven, then top with whipped cream mixed with a little honey, for a sweet.

BANANA PUFFS

Preheat oven to 500°F.

Combine	2 cups mashed, cooked sweet potatoes
and	1 large, ripe banana, mashed
Beat in	2 tbs melted butter
	1 egg yolk
	1 tsp salt
	$\frac{1}{3}$ cup hot milk or cream
	$\frac{1}{8}$ tsp nutmeg
	$\frac{1}{8}$ tsp ginger
In another bowl, beat until stiff	1 egg white

Fold it lightly into the potato mixture. Drop the batter in tablespoonfuls, well apart, on to a greased cookie sheet, or place the mixture in buttered muffin tins. Bake the puffs for about 12 minutes or until lightly browned.

SAMBALS FOR CURRY

The ceremony of serving the Javanese dish, *rijsttafel*, or rice table as it is commonly known, is part of its charm, and bananas are an integral part of any rice table. In Java, one refers to the meal by the number of separate dishes involved: as a 'one boy curry' or a 'twenty-two boy curry', each boy representing one dish. The rice is passed first and spread generously over your plate forming the base for the 'table'. The meat or vegetable curry dishes come next and should be generously spooned over the rice. Now for the crowning touch: the boys bring onion rings, chopped egg, chopped raisins, grated nuts, grated coconut, relish, chutney, preserved ginger, pickles and bananas in any number of forms — halves of fried bananas, banana chips broken into pieces, or plain, freshly chopped banana sprinkled with lemon juice, for example. You cut through the dish to eat it, and enjoy a feast.

PLANTAIN TAMALES

Boil until tender	3 ripe plantains
in	salted water
Mash with fork and add	2 tbs shortening
	$\frac{1}{2}$ cup sugar
	$\frac{1}{4}$ tsp grated nutmeg
	$\frac{1}{2}$ tsp cinnamon
	a little flour

Wash some plantain leaves, tearing away midribs, and cut into 6-inch square pieces. Put a spoonful of mixture on each square. Tie in a small parcel. Drop into boiling water and cook for 5–10 minutes.

BANANA TORTILLA
(from Central America)

Bake whole green plantains in their skins until soft in a medium oven for about 45 minutes, longer if plantains are large. When soft, peel and smash each one flat on a board covered with a little flour. Fry these flattened patties in hot oil to crisp. Serve hot.

This recipe was a gift from Maria Esterbrook at the Rota Naval Air Station in 1979.

SALADS

CHICKEN SALAD HAWAIIAN

For 6 servings:

Combine in bowl
     3 cups cooked chicken breast
     1 cup chopped celery
     1 cup grated or flaked coconut

(For guests who prefer to eat without additional sugar, use dried, dessicated coconut or grate a fresh one for this dish.)

Add
     $\frac{1}{3}$ cup blanched almonds or walnut pieces
     3 tbs sesame seeds
     3 cups cubed fresh pineapple
     3 medium bananas, cut in chunks and dipped in lemon juice

Toss lightly in a dressing of
     $\frac{1}{2}$ cup pineapple juice
     $\frac{1}{2}$ cup mayonnaise
     2 tbs sesame seeds

This can be served in the pineapple shells for a festive dish. For 6 persons, just cut the pineapple into 6 wedges before removing fruit. Then cut fruit carefully away from the skin, reserving skin (with leaves still attached, if possible) to use as a dish for serving the salad on. Arrange on your prettiest plate or in a wooden bowl.

TROPICAL SALAD

Peel a quantity of green plantains. You will have to use a paring knife and peel as you would potatoes, for green plantains do not give up their skin readily. Boil the plantains as you would potatoes. Cool. Dice.

Mix together	4 cups cooked, cubed green plantains
	2 tbs chopped onion
	1 cup diced celery
	2 tbs diced green pepper
	2 tbs pimento strips
	2 tsp prepared mustard
	$\frac{1}{4}$ cup mayonnaise
	$\frac{1}{4}$ cup vegetable oil
	1 tsp coarse pepper
	1 tsp salt

Serve chilled and decorate with slices of hard-boiled egg and strips of green pepper, if desired. Makes 6 generous servings.

NUTTY PEANUT SALAD

Mix together	1 tbs vinegar
	2 tbs cornstarch
	$\frac{1}{2}$ cup water
	$\frac{1}{2}$ cup sugar
Add	1 heaped tbs butter or margarine

Cook over low heat until it begins to thicken.

Pour in very slowly	2 beaten egg yolks

Cook until creamy. Refrigerate.

Peel and slice	3 whole bananas
Layer with	1 cup Spanish peanuts

Then add a layer of sauce. Repeat until all ingredients are used up. Chill at least 30 minutes.

This is good with both hot and cold dishes.

FRUIT SALAD BUFFET

A fun salad lunch is one of fruit, offered in a mix-your-own salad manner.

Take a large tray and line it with grape leaves or large, flat lettuce leaves. In the centre, place a shallow dish piled high with heart of lettuce pieces, watercress, or spikes of endive hearts. Then, around this dish, arrange fruits according to your liking, such as:

apples, unpeeled, cut in eighths
bananas, split and quartered
cantaloupe or honeydew melon, peeled, cut in crescents
cherries, pitted
grapefruit sections
orange sections
pears, unpeeled, cut in eighths
pineapple spears, or half-rounds
raspberries
strawberries
watermelon, seeded, cut in wedges

Decorate the tray with mint or parsley. Flank it with bowls of various fruit-salad dressings. Let each guest compile his own salad and add his choice of dressing.

FRUIT 'N NUT SALAD

Combine

1 head romaine or other crisp lettuce,
   torn into bite-sized pieces
2 sliced bananas
$\frac{1}{2}$ cup raisins
$\frac{1}{3}$ cup chopped walnuts
1 small, sliced apple

Just before serving, toss with an oil and vinegar dressing or Double Fruit Salad Dressing*. Makes 6 servings.

BANANA WALDORF SALAD

Bananas, apples and oranges make a very good salad when you add chopped celery and mayonnaise and decorate the salad with the yellow blooms we have on aloes plants (locally called sempervivy). Everyone knows the stalk of the sempervivy has a bitter taste, but the pretty yellow blossom is crisp, slightly sweet and very pleasant on top of a banana fruit salad. The tastiest flowers are the ones that have not yet opened at the bottom. This is a West Indian Waldorf Salad!

FROZEN BANANA SALAD (1)

Combine
4 mashed bananas
1 cup crushed pineapple
1 tbs lemon juice
6-oz jar maraschino cherries, drained
    and finely chopped
$\frac{1}{2}$ cup chopped pecans
$\frac{3}{4}$ cup sugar
1 tsp salt

Mix well. Pour into 9-inch square pan. Freeze. Remove from freezer 10 minutes before serving. Cut into squares. Serve on crisp lettuce, with or without dressing. Yields 9 servings.

FROZEN BANANA SALAD (2)

Oil a 5-cup mould or bowl.
Combine
2 cups sour cream
20-oz can crushed pineapple, with juice
2 mashed bananas
$\frac{3}{4}$ cup sugar
$\frac{1}{2}$ cup chopped nuts
2 tbs chopped maraschino cherries

Freeze. Unmould 15 minutes before serving. Serves 10.

CARIBBEAN FRUIT SALAD

Slice
6 mangoes
5 avocados
5 oranges
3 lemons
3 bananas
1 pawpaw (papaya)

Squeeze juice from
1 mango
1 orange
1 lemon

Make a syrup with
2 cups rum
$1\frac{1}{2}$ cups sugar

Coat the sliced fruit with this syrup and let it sit for a long time to marinate before serving.

PINEANA DRESSING

For a fresh fruit salad, this is the easiest of dressings, and very tasty.

Mix together in a
blender   1 cup pineapple juice
                            1 medium-ripe banana
                            1 tbs lemon juice

Use also as a dip for chunks of fresh fruit. Alternatively, substitute your favourite fruit juice. For a truly special dip, mix in a small carton of sour cream just before serving.

DOUBLE FRUIT SALAD DRESSING

For a fresh fruit salad, this is very tasty and quick to make.

In a blender, whip   1 small carton cottage cheese
Add   ½ cup orange or other juice,
                                unsweetened
                       1 medium banana in chunks

Do not overwhip, merely mix banana and juice in. When mixture is consistency for dipping, remove to a pretty glass bowl and use as a dressing for fruit salad, or as a dip for chunks of fresh fruit.
Alternatively, choose your favourite fruit juice, such as peach for a salad with peaches, pineapple with pineapple salad, etc.

PINEAPPLE BANANA STRAWBERRY JELLO

Dissolve   2 pkgs strawberry jello
in   2 cups boiling water
Chill until it begins to thicken.
Add and stir in well   2 pkgs frozen strawberries
                       2–3 bananas, mashed
                       1 medium can crushed pineapple and
                             juice
Refrigerate until set.

PIES FOR PUDDINGS

VENETIAN BANANA RASPBERRY TART

Combine	¾ cup sugar
with	1 tbs quick-cooking tapioca
Stir in	¾ cup crushed frozen or fresh raspberries
	¾ cup crushed banana

Let stand for 15 minutes. Then, stir over heat until mixture boils. Remove from heat. Let stand 20 minutes. Cover and chill.

Turn chilled mixture into	9-inch pastry shell, baked and cooled
Beat to soft peaks	1 cup whipping cream
with	2 tbs sugar

Spread cream over banana/berry mixture.

Add layers of	1 cup fresh raspberries
	1 cup sliced banana

To prepare meringue:

Beat until frothy	2 egg whites
Gradually add	½ cup sifted, powdered sugar

Beat until stiff peaks form. Spread meringue on top of fruit, sealing edges. Grill 3–4 inches from heat for 1–2 minutes. Serve at once.

BANANA PARFAIT PIE

Prepare butter crust:

Soften and cream	½ cup butter
with	2 tbs sugar
Add	1 cup flour

Mix until dough forms. Press dough into 9-inch pan with your fingers, reserving a quarter of mixture for crumbs for topping. Bake crust at 375°F for 10–12 minutes, or until just golden-brown.

Parfait filling:

Combine	⅔ cup sugar
	¼ cup lemon juice
	1 unbeaten egg-white

Beat at high speed until soft peaks form.

Separately, beat	1 cup whipping cream

When thick, fold in egg-white mixture by hand. Spoon half of filling into baked crust.

Slice and add	2–3 bananas
Spoon over	2–3 tbs banana jam, or similar jam

Cover with remaining filling. Sprinkle on reserved crumbs. Chill until quite firm.

BANANA SPLIT PIE

Soften	½ cup butter
Gradually add	1½ cups confectioner's sugar

Cream well.

Add	2 eggs, one at a time

Beat well after each addition.

Add	1 tsp vanilla
Slice	2 bananas
Sprinkle with	1 tbs lemon juice
Grate	1 square chocolate

Fold bananas and chocolate into sugar/butter/egg mixture.

Pour into	8-inch pie shell, baked and cooled
Garnish with	½ cup chopped walnuts
	more banana slices

Chill 2–3 hours and serve.

FRUIT CREAM PIE

Sift together	1 cup flour
	$\frac{1}{2}$ tsp salt
Cut in	$\frac{1}{3}$ cup margarine or shortening
Sprinkle on	3–4 tbs cold water

Toss lightly with fork until dough is moist enough to hold together. Form into a ball. Roll out on floured board to $1\frac{1}{2}$ inches larger than a 9-inch pie pan. Fit pastry loosely into pan, and make a standing edge. Prick crust with fork and bake in 450°F oven for 10–12 minutes.

Fruit Cream Filling:

Combine	1 cup canned, sliced, drained peaches
	$\frac{1}{2}$ cup chopped dates
	$\frac{1}{2}$ cup miniature marshmallows
	$1\frac{1}{4}$ cups sliced bananas
	3 tbs lemon juice
	3 tbs honey

Chill thoroughly.

Whip	$\frac{1}{2}$ cup whipping cream

Fold in fruit mixture. Pour into cooled, baked crust.

Sprinkle with	2 tbs crushed cheese crackers

Chill until ready to serve.

From a recipe by Mrs L. Huber, Ste. Genevieve, Missouri.

OLD FASHIONED BANANA CREAM PIE

Mix together in a *saucepan*	2 tbs flour
	2 tbs cornstarch
	$\frac{1}{2}$ tsp salt
	$\frac{2}{3}$ cup sugar
Stir in	2 cups milk

Bring to a boil over low heat. Cook until thickened, stirring constantly.

Stir in	1 tsp vanilla
	1 tbs butter

This home-cooked sauce takes longer but makes a better pudding, and it has staying power — it does not turn watery like the instant pudding mix.

At this point, you have an option — either to prepare Old Fashioned Banana Pudding with Vanilla Wafers*, or pour your filling into a pie shell.

For a pie: cool filling slightly, then pour into a 9-inch baked pastry shell that has been lined with sliced bananas.

To make meringue:

Beat until frothy	3 egg whites
Add	$\frac{1}{4}$ tsp cream of tartar

Continue beating until stiff enough to hold a peak.

Gradually beat in	2 tbs powdered sugar per egg white

Beat until meringue is stiff and glossy. Pile meringue on top of cooled pie, making sure it touches the edges of the pastry to prevent it from shrinking. With back of tablespoon, swirl large, graceful curls. Bake at 425°F until delicately brown, for about 5–6 minutes. Just before serving, press more banana slices between meringue and pastry edge.

BANANA CUSTARD CREAM PIE

Mix in a saucepan	1 pkg banana pudding mix (non instant)
	1 cup evaporated milk
	2 beaten egg yolks
	1 cup water

Cook over medium heat until mixture boils and thickens, about 5 minutes. Cool. Pour into baked pie shell. Cover with meringue:

Beat until frothy	2 egg whites
Add	2 tbs powdered sugar
Beat until stiff, fold in	2 tbs powdered sugar

Bake on centre rack of oven for 7–8 minutes at 400°F, or until meringue is light-brown. Cool thoroughly before serving.

BANANA MARSHMALLOW PIE

Prepare	1 pkg vanilla instant pudding
Line	8-inch baked pastry shell
with	2–3 sliced bananas

Pour prepared pudding into pastry shell.

Top pie with	2 cups miniature marshmallows

Grill top until lightly golden-brown. Chill. Serve only when thoroughly chilled.

FLUFFY BANANA CREAM PIE

In a small bowl, blend	1 pkg instant vanilla-pudding and pie-filling mix

with	1 envelope whipped topping mix
	1½ cups milk
	½ tsp vanilla

Use low speed of mixer to blend, then increase speed to high and beat until very thick, about 3 minutes.

Prepare either an uncooked pie crust (using Graham Crackers) or a cooked one with flour, shortening and water. Pour a third of mixture into prepared crust. Layer slices of one large banana on top. Pour remaining filling over banana. Chill about half an hour, or until set. Garnish with an additional sliced banana and topping, if desired. Makes one pie.

Note: To prevent garnish from darkening, dip banana slices in lemon juice.

EASY BANANA SOUR CREAM PIE

Layer bottom of baked,	
9-inch pie shell with	1 (3¾ oz) pkg vanilla instant pudding
mixed with	1 cup milk
and	1 cup sour cream
	2–3 sliced bananas
Top with	½ pint Cool Whip or other whipped topping
Sprinkle on	¼ cup chopped pecans

Chill at least 4 hours before serving.

BANANA CHEESE PIE

Beat until fluffy	8-oz pkg cream cheese
with	¾ cup light-brown sugar
	1 tsp cinnamon
	1 tsp freshly grated nutmeg
	1 tsp ground ginger
Add	3 eggs

Beat well after each addition.

Stir in	1 cup mashed banana
	1 cup evaporated milk
	1 tsp vanilla

Pour into unbaked 9-inch pie shell. Bake at 375°F for about 45–50 minutes, or until knife comes out clean when inserted. Chill. Serve with whipped cream.

NO-BAKE BANANA PIE

In heavy saucepan, mix	1 envelope unflavoured gelatin
	1 tsp freshly ground nutmeg
	1 tsp cinnamon
	1 tsp ginger
Add	$\frac{1}{4}$ cup water

Heat slowly, until gelatin dissolves.

Add	1 can sweetened condensed milk
	2 well-beaten eggs

Mix well, and continue cooking over low heat for about 5 minutes.
Mixture will thicken slightly.

Remove from heat and	
stir in	2 cups mashed bananas

Pour mixture into Graham Cracker or pre-baked regular crust. Serve
with dollops of whipped cream.

LIGHT LEMON BANANA CREAM PIE

Bake	9-inch pie crust
Meanwhile, in a bowl,	
mix together	1 can sweetened condensed milk
	$\frac{1}{2}$ cup whipped cream
	pulp of 1 lemon (peeled, cut in small pieces)
	3 tbs lemon juice
	1 tsp grated lemon rind
In a separate bowl,	
dissolve	1 envelope gelatin
in	$\frac{1}{2}$ cup hot water

Cool slightly, then pour into lemon cream mixture. Mix well. Pour a
layer of this custard into baked, cooled pie crust.

Slice	1 large or 2 medium bananas

Lay banana on custard, then pour on remaining custard.

Top custard with	2 cups whipped cream, or non-dairy frozen topping

Great! But to make it pretty as well as tasty, decorate the pie with
thin slices of lemon cut in quarters and/or sliced bananas dipped in
lemon juice.

FRUIT COBBLER
('Cobble-up' means to mix in a hurry.)

Prepare half given recipe of Banana Shortcake* dough.

Heat together	2 cups diced bananas
	$\frac{1}{2}$ cup orange juice
	2 tbs sugar
	1 tbs cornstarch
Mixed with	2 tbs water

Pour fruit mixture into a 2-quart baking dish. Dot with butter. Cover with spoonfuls of basic shortcake dough. Bake at 400°F for 20 minutes.

BANANA PUDDING TORTE

Mix until crumbly	1$\frac{1}{2}$ cups flour
	1$\frac{1}{2}$ sticks margarine
Add	$\frac{1}{2}$ cup chopped nuts

Press into pan, 9×13 inches. Bake at 375°F for 15 minutes. Cool.

Beat together until fluffy	8-oz pkg cream cheese
	1 cup confectioner's sugar
Fold in	$\frac{1}{2}$ large carton Cool Whip or 1$\frac{1}{2}$ cups whipped cream

Spread over crust.

Combine	2 3-oz pkgs instant banana pudding mix
	3 cups milk

Beat until thickened. Spread over cream cheese mixture.

Spread on	remaining $\frac{1}{2}$ carton Cool Whip or 1$\frac{1}{2}$ cups whipped cream
Sprinkle on	$\frac{1}{2}$ cup chopped nuts

Refrigerate at least 3 hours, or overnight. Keep in a cool place. Serves 12.

PINEANA PIE

Reserve	2–3 tbs crushed pineapple
Mix together	8-oz pkg cream cheese
	1 cup crushed pineapple, drained

Beat with mixer until light and fluffy.

Fold in	large carton whipped topping mix
Then carefully fold in	2 medium bananas, sliced

Turn into	9-inch pie crust

Decorate with more banana slices and reserved crushed pineapple.

BANANA DAIQUIRI PIE

In a double boiler,

blend	$\frac{1}{2}$ cup sugar
	$\frac{1}{4}$ cup flour
	3–4 egg yolks

Cream together until light.

Add	1 pint scalded milk

Put over boiling water and stir until mixture comes to a boil. Remove from heat. Stir frequently until cool.

Add	2 thinly sliced bananas
	$\frac{1}{4}$ cup rum
	2 tbs lime juice
Pour into	9-inch baked pie shell

Serve plain, or with whipped cream, or whipped non-dairy topping. Can be used as a filling between cake layers, or as a topping for wedges of cake. Without the pie crust, it also makes a nice pudding.

BANANA CHEESECAKE

Beat	2 eggs
Add and beat well	$\frac{1}{4}$ cup dry, powdered milk
	$\frac{3}{4}$ cup sugar
	$\frac{1}{2}$ cup sour cream
	2 cups soft or cream cheese
	1 tbs banana liqueur
	1 medium mashed banana

Pour into prepared cookie or Graham Cracker crust. Bake at 350°F for 20 minutes.

Mix together	$\frac{1}{2}$ cup sour cream
	$\frac{1}{4}$ cup sugar
	$\frac{1}{2}$ mashed banana
	1 tsp banana liqueur

Pour over hot filling. Return to oven. Bake 10 minutes more. Cool for at least 6 hours before serving.

MORE PUDDINGS

BANANAS BRÛLÉE

You'll get rave reviews when you serve this winner. And besides tasting good it is easy to make.

In a bowl, beat together	2 3-oz pkgs cream cheese
When fluffy, add	1 cup dairy sour cream
	2 tbs brown sugar

Beat until completely smooth.

Slice	5–6 medium bananas
Reserve	$\frac{1}{2}$ banana

Put a layer of cream cheese mixture in a shallow 8-inch round heat-proof dish. Use about a quarter of mixture.

Sprinkle on	2–3 tbs brown sugar

Layer on some bananas, then more sugar until you have used up all the bananas. Spoon rest of cheese mixture over bananas.

Sieve evenly over top	$\frac{1}{4}$ cup brown sugar

Grill 4–5 inches from heat for 1–2 minutes, or until sugar turns golden-brown. Slice reserved banana-half over top of dessert. Serve immediately.

BANANA SURPRISE

Beat together with a mixer for 2 minutes	2 eggs
	2 cups powdered sugar
	2 sticks butter
Meanwhile, mix together	2 cups crushed Graham Crackers or digestive biscuits
	1 stick butter

Pat mixture into a 13×9×2 inch pan.

Cover crust with	2 medium bananas, sliced
Drain well and pour on	1⅔ cups crushed pineapple
Spread on	1 small carton whipped topping mix
Or spoon on	2 cups stiffly whipped cream, lightly sweetened
Sprinkle with	½ cup chopped walnuts
Optionally, dot with	¼ cup cherry halves

This should be made a day ahead, as the flavour improves with time. It is an elegant, rich dessert, and, in fact, it is so good, one guest said anything this good had to be sinful.

OLD FASHIONED BANANA PUDDING WITH VANILLA WAFERS

Mom always served this at holiday time, often as an extra dessert. It wasn't quick and easy to make then, because she had to make her pudding from scratch, separating and beating the eggs, folding a little of the hot cornstarch, milk and sugar mixture into some of the eggs before returning them to the pan — so the eggs wouldn't curdle — she told me. Even today, her version is better (see filling for Old Fashioned Banana Cream Pie*). These days you can use boxed mixes and instant pudding, but unless you plan to eat it soon after it is made, don't use an instant mix or it will turn watery.

Prepare one box of instant vanilla pudding according to directions on the label but reduce the liquid to three-quarters of the amount called for, probably 1½ cups instead of 2. Allow to cool slightly. Now line a pretty serving dish with vanilla wafers or cookies and slice on a layer of bananas. Pour on some of the pudding. Repeat until all of the pudding has been used up. Chill thoroughly before serving with or without whipped cream or whipped topping.
Try also Banana Daiquiri Pie* filling for a nice pudding.

MARSHMALLOW BANANA PUDDING

Prepare   1 pkg vanilla pudding
Remove from heat.
Stir in   1 cup miniature marshmallows
                             1 sliced banana

Chill. Top with banana slices and decorate with whipped cream.

CANDIED BANANA FRITTERS
(Taiwanese)

Beat   1 egg
Add   3 tbs flour
                             3 tbs cornstarch
                             1 tbs water

Mix together to make an egg paste.
Peel   3 bananas

Cut each into eight pieces. Coat each piece with egg paste. Deep fry
for 15 seconds, frying each piece separately. Remove fruit and drain.
Reheat oil.
In another pan, heat   2 tbs oil
Add   6 tbs sugar

Stir over moderate heat until sugar melts. Deep fry banana pieces
again. When melted sugar turns golden-brown, add fruit and 2
tablespoons fried sesame seeds. Serve fritters on a plate that has been
coated with oil and heated. Fritters must be piping hot when they
reach the table of eagerly awaiting guests.
Serve with a bowl of ice water containing floating ice cubes. Each
guest (hopefully using chopsticks) picks up a fritter and dips it into the
bowl of ice water to solidify the sugar and make eating easier. If
chopsticks are out of the question, provide bamboo skewers so that
guests can spear the fritter, dip it into the water and eat.
Two apples may be substituted for bananas.
See also Banana Fritters*.

BANANA LUMPIA
(from the Philippines)

Street vendors are popular in the Philippines, and one of our
favourites was the lumpia vendor, who had a wok, set on bricks over a
charcoal fire. In the wok was very hot oil. He, or she, would unpeel a
banana and break it into natural sections (see Hints*). If the banana

was a large one, she'd cut each section in two; if small, she'd use it whole. She wrapped each piece of banana in a lumpia wrapper (available in the frozen food section as egg-roll skin), carefully folding it envelope fashion. She then tossed the package into the hot oil and spooned a scant teaspoon of brown sugar directly on top of it in the oil. The oil cooked the wrapper to a golden brown, while it melted the sugar into a syrup which enveloped the lumpia as it was lifted out of the oil with a slotted spoon. It was handed to us directly, scalding hot. The vendor laughed at us as we tossed it back and forth from hand to hand. But once we bit into that succulent, natural flavour, we declared it had been worth waiting for.

BAKED BANANAS (1)

In a baking dish, smear	2 tbs butter
Peel	8 small or 4 large bananas
Arrange in buttered dish.	
Mix and pour on	$\frac{1}{4}-\frac{1}{2}$ cup dry white wine
	$\frac{1}{3}-\frac{1}{2}$ cup honey
	1 tbs lemon juice
Sprinkle on	$\frac{1}{2}$ tsp cinnamon
Dot with	2 tbs butter

(This recipe can be prepared up to this stage, refrigerated, and baked several hours or even a day or two later.)
Heat oven to 375°F. Put baking dish on middle level and bake for 20–25 minutes. Baste every 5 minutes or so with the liquid in the dish. You can also bake ahead and reheat, or flambé the dish.
To flame the bananas:
Be sure the baked bananas are bubbling hot.

Sprinkle on	1 tbs granulated sugar
Pour on	$\frac{1}{4}-\frac{1}{2}$ cup cognac

Avert your face, light the cognac with a match, and spoon it over the bananas until the flames die down. Serve on hot plates.

BAKED BANANAS (2)
(a sweeter version)

Peel and slice in half lengthwise	4 bananas
Place in baking dish.	
Combine in bowl	$\frac{1}{4}$ cup brown sugar
	1 tbs butter

Then add $\frac{1}{2}$ cup orange juice
                              $\frac{1}{4}$ tsp nutmeg
                              $\frac{1}{2}-\frac{3}{4}$ cup rum

Heat mixture and pour over bananas. Baste frequently with juice while baking for 25–30 minutes at 375°F. Just before serving, pour on a little more rum. If you want to be really festive, heat the additional rum before pouring over the bananas. Light and pour over baked bananas while still flaming.

BANANAS CARIBBEAN
In the above recipe for Baked Bananas, just before you put the pan into the oven for baking, sprinkle on $\frac{1}{2}$ cup grated fresh coconut.

CANDIED BAKED BANANAS

Preheat oven to 375°F.
In a small saucepan
combine $\frac{1}{3}$ cup dark-brown sugar
                              $\frac{1}{2}$ cup water

Bring to a boil. Lower heat, simmer 5 minutes.
Peel   2 slightly underripe bananas

Slice them in half lengthwise, then slice in half crosswise. Place the 4 pieces of cut banana in a shallow, buttered baking dish.
Sprinkle with $\frac{1}{4}$ tsp salt
To the cooled syrup, add   juice of $\frac{1}{2}$ lemon or 1 lime

Pour syrup over bananas. Bake about 30 minutes, turning fruit after first 15 minutes. Serve on hot plates, sprinkled with rum and chopped candied ginger.

GLAZED BANANAS

Slice bananas in half lengthwise, with peel intact. Place skin side down in shallow baking pan.
Melt over low heat $\frac{1}{4}$ cup guava or apple jelly
Stir in   2 tbs lime juice

Brush half the mixture over the bananas. Bake in 375°F oven for 8–10 minutes. Remove from oven. Brush with remaining glaze. Makes 4 servings.

WEST INDIAN FLAMING BANANAS

Sauté   banana halves or sections
in   butter

Cook over medium flame until bananas are browned.

Sprinkle on	brown sugar
	sliced almonds
	raisins
In another pan heat	$\frac{1}{4}$ cup rum

Set rum alight and pour over the bananas.

SWEET FRIED BANANAS

Mix as little water as possible into some brown sugar to make a syrup.
For each 2 tbs of syrup:

Add	$\frac{1}{2}$ tsp honey
	$\frac{1}{2}$ tsp concentrated orange juice

Slice bananas lengthwise and soak in syrup for an hour. Then fry lightly in butter, pouring the syrup over the bananas from time to time.

BANANAS FOSTER

Somehow, bananas that had been sautéd in butter, then flamed in liquor and served with ice-cream were given the name of Bananas Foster, and this dish can be found on many a fancy menu. With or without its name, it is a fine dessert, one that is quick and easy to prepare, yet elegant in that it is served flaming, and it is also very good to eat.

Melt in a flambé pan or	
heavy skillet	6 tbs butter
Add	$1\frac{1}{2}$ cups brown sugar
	$\frac{3}{4}$ tsp cinnamon
	$\frac{1}{3}$ cup banana liqueur

Stir to mix and cook for a few minutes.

Add to the sauce	6 peeled bananas, split lengthwise
Pour on	$\frac{1}{3}$ cup dark rum

Do *not* stir rum in. Allow all to heat well then tip the pan so that the flame from the burner catches the sauce (or use a match). Allow this sauce to flame until it dies out by itself and tip the pan with a circular motion to prolong the flaming.

Place a scoop of vanilla ice-cream in a dessert dish. Carefully lift the bananas out of the pan. Place 3–4 pieces over each portion of ice-cream. Then spoon the hot sauce from the pan over the top and serve at once.

BANANAS IN RUM SAUCE

Peel   3–4 ripe bananas
Cut into ½-inch cubes. Chill.
Beat together until
double in volume   4 egg yolks
                               ¾ cup superfine sugar

Beat to soft peaks   2 egg whites
To the egg yolk
mixture, add   4 tbs white rum

Fold in beaten whites. Serve immediately, spooning rum sauce over bananas in individual serving dishes. Sprinkle with freshly grated nutmeg.

BANANAS AU RHUM

Melt in large saucepan   2 tbs butter
Split lengthwise   4 peeled bananas
Brown bananas in butter.
Sprinkle on   4 tbs rum
                               2 tbs dark-brown sugar

Cover and cook 3 minutes. Remove from heat. Spoon liquid over bananas. Serve hot or cold.

BANANAS FLAMBÉ ANTIGUA

Set oven at 400°F. Pierce unpeeled bananas and bake for 10–15 minutes, or until skin is dark. Remove from oven. Lay each banana flat, slice skin around the middle, lengthwise, and remove top half of skin only.

In a heat-proof baking
dish, melt   4 tbs butter
Add   ½ tsp grated allspice

Lay the bananas, flesh downwards on the mixture. Carefully remove the remaining skin.

Sprinkle on   ¼ cup lime juice
In a separate pan, warm   ¼ cup high proof rum

Set it aflame with a match and pour over bananas. Baste until the flame dies out and serve to eagerly waiting guests.

MIXED FRUIT FLAMBÉ

Drain	8-oz can sliced peaches, retaining juice
Section	2 medium oranges

Collect orange juice and add to peach juice. If necessary, add additional fruit juice to make $\frac{3}{4}$ cup.

Combine in a pan	1 tbs cornstarch
with	1 tsp allspice for sweets
Stir in	$\frac{3}{4}$ cup reserved juice
	1 tbs lemon juice

Cook, stirring occasionally, over medium heat until thick. Remove from heat.

Stir in	peaches and orange segments
	1 small, sliced banana
	$\frac{1}{4}$ cup raisins

Heat through, gently.

In a small saucepan,	
warm	$\frac{1}{4}$ cup brandy

Ignite and pour into fruit sauce. Stir. Ladle sauce over ice-cream, pound-cake, or into dessert dishes.

PHILIPPINE STEWED BANANAS

Peel some underripe bananas and slice in half lengthwise. Layer in a heavy pot with $\frac{1}{4}$ cup of brown sugar for each large banana. Add $\frac{1}{2}$ cup of water to the pot. Bring to a boil. Cover. Reduce heat and simmer, shaking occasionally, but do not stir. Shake the pot from side to side and up and down every few minutes to prevent burning. Serve for dessert just as it is, or pour on a jigger of rum, or top with whipped cream.

RICE PUDDING WITH BANANAS AND RAISINS

Rice pudding has been part of our family staple diet as long as I can remember — but we had more than one kind. Like any good cook, my mother varied her offering with whatever was available in the larder, and rice pudding was the dessert served when she was out of almost everything else — like her Vinegar Pie it could always be made from pantry contents. But there were two versions of rice pudding which she served the most: this regular, stick-to-the-ribs rice pudding, as a family dessert, and Fluffy Whipped Cream Rice Pudding*, for 'company'.

Preheat oven to 325°F. Use leftover rice, or prepare rice ahead so it can be cooled.

To	2 cups cooked rice
add and combine	1¼ cups milk
	4–6 tbs sugar (especially dark-brown), molasses or honey
	1 tbs butter
	1 tsp vanilla
	2–4 eggs (2 are satisfactory but 4 make it lighter)
	grated rind of 1 lemon (optional)
	1 tsp lemon juice
	½ cup raisins
	½ cup chopped banana, not too ripe

Grease a baking dish and cover the bottom and sides of the dish with rolled crumbs of cookies, stale bread, crackers or whatever you have. Pour in rice mixture, then top with more crumbs. Bake for about 50 minutes, or until set. Serve hot or cold, with or without sauce.

FLUFFY WHIPPED CREAM RICE PUDDING

Mix	2 tsp gelatin
with	¼ cup cold water

Heat until dissolved.

Add	1 cup cooked rice
	¼ cup sugar, or other sweetening
	¼ cup chopped nuts

Chill.

Whip until stiff	2 cups chilled whipping cream
Fold in	2 tsp vanilla
then	rice mixture

Place in a wet mould and chill at least half a day. (Mom used to cover it well, put it in a covered bucket and set in the nearby spring.) When set, unmould and serve plain, or with a sauce of your choice.

FRUIT SAUCE

Mix and heat to boiling point	1 cup unsweetened fruit juice
	½ cup sugar, or other sweetener
Blend	2 tbs cornstarch
with	4 tbs cold water

Stir into heated fruit juice in a slow fashion, stirring all the while so lumps do not form. Remove from heat.

Stir in	2 tbs lemon juice
	2 tbs butter
If desired, add	1 cup chopped fruit (banana is very good)

HOT WINE SA`ICE
(for special occasions)

Cream	$\frac{1}{2}$ cup butter
	1 cup sugar
Beat and add	1–2 eggs
Stir in	$\frac{3}{4}$ cup wine, rum, or similar

Heat thoroughly just before serving. Do not boil or let burn.

BANANA PUDDING
(from Israel)

Cube	$\frac{1}{3}$ loaf stale bread

Put this into a buttered baking dish.

Sprinkle on	$\frac{1}{3}$ cup raw or brown sugar
Dot with	2 tbs butter
Sprinkle on	$\frac{1}{3}$ cup honey or jam
	$\frac{1}{3}$ cup raisins (or any dried fruit)
	$\frac{1}{3}$ cup chopped nuts
Slice on	5–6 bananas
Beat	4–5 eggs
with	3–4 cups milk

Pour over ingredients in bowl. Let mixture set, refrigerated for about an hour. Bake at 375°F for 35 minutes, or until knife when inserted comes out clean. May be served hot or cold, with or without whipped cream or whipped non-dairy topping.

Apples may be substituted for bananas.

SUPER BANANA CRISP

Place in 10×6 inch baking dish	4 cups peeled, sliced bananas
In a bowl, combine	$\frac{2}{3}$ cup packed brown sugar
	$\frac{1}{2}$ cup flour
	$\frac{1}{2}$ cup old-fashioned oats
	1 tsp cinnamon

Cut into small pieces
and mix together $\frac{1}{2}$ lb pasteurised processed cheese
$\frac{1}{3}$ cup butter
$\frac{1}{2}$ cup nuts

Sprinkle mixture over bananas. Bake at 350°F for 30 minutes. Serve plain, or, if desired, with whipped cream.

BANANA TIPSY CAKE

A custardy, chilled dessert with a sherry, fruit flavour, something like an English trifle.

Combine $1\frac{1}{2}$ cups biscuit mix
$\frac{3}{4}$ cup sugar
3 tbs soft butter
1 egg
$\frac{3}{4}$ cup light cream, or half cream and
    half evaporated milk
1 tsp vanilla

Beat until well blended and smooth. Pour into greased and floured 8×8×2 inch pan. Bake at 350°F for 35–40 minutes. Do not overbake. Cool. Cut cake into 16 pieces. Slice each piece in half, horizontally.
Spread slices with banana jam, or similar
Arrange like sandwiches in 11×7×1$\frac{1}{2}$ inch glass dish.
Sprinkle with $\frac{1}{3}$ cup sherry
Pour on 1 pkg vanilla pudding mix made up with
    $\frac{1}{2}$ cup extra milk
Layer with sliced bananas
Sprinkle with $\frac{1}{3}$ cup toasted slivered almonds
Top with $\frac{3}{4}$ cup whipping cream (whipped and
    sweetened with low calorie sweetener,
    if desired)

Chill well.

BANANA AMBROSIA

Peel and thinly slice 1 orange
Peel and slice 2 ripe bananas
Measure $\frac{3}{4}$ cup coconut
2 tbs powdered sugar

Arrange alternate layers of orange and banana in a serving dish or parfait glasses, sprinkling each layer with some of the coconut and sugar. See also Banana-Stuffed Papaya*.

FRUIT COMPOTE

Cut into sections a
selection of   grapefruit
                             oranges
                             apples
                             bananas

Using your prettiest glassware, layer fruit in individual serving dishes.
Drizzle Grand Marnier over all. Chill. Serve.

FRESH FRUITS IN GRAND MARNIER SAUCE

Good old fruit-salad is even better when prepared this way. Fruit
salad is acceptable at any time, as long as it is made with good-quality
fruit and the fruits used have an affinity with each other. The banana
is an essential ingredient in any fruit salad and is almost always
available, as are apples, oranges and grapefruit. Add any other fruits
available.

Peel, dice and combine
in a salad bowl   3 navel oranges
                             1 large, ripe banana
                             1 crisp apple
                             1 grapefruit
If available, add   1 cup white seedless grapes
                             1 cup small whole strawberries
Sprinkle on   2 tbs sugar
and, if desired   2 tbs kirsch

Cover and refrigerate until serving time.

Meanwhile, in the top
of a double boiler,
combine   4 egg yolks
                             1 tsp cornstarch
                             $\frac{1}{2}$ cup sugar

Beat until a pale-yellow colour.
Add   1 cup warm milk

Set over simmering water. Whisk constantly until mixture is thick
enough to coat a heavy spoon. Do not let it boil! When custard is
done, strain into a serving bowl.
Add $\frac{1}{4}$ cup Grand Marnier
                             1 tsp vanilla
                             1 tsp grated orange rind

Cool completely, then refrigerate 2–3 hours.

Just before serving,
whisk into sauce   ½ cup heavy cream, whipped
Drain fruit salad of accumulated juice, pour the sauce over the fruit
and serve immediately.
This sauce can also be used over Baked Bananas*.

FRUIT BALLS

Remove membrane from 2 medium oranges but leave white inner part
of the peel. Wash the peel and steam it for 15 minutes. This should
remove some bitterness. Grind coarsely. Makes about one cup of peel.

Wash and soak   1 cup dried apricots
                         1 cup raisins
After a few minutes, drain and chop coarsely.
Dice   1 medium banana
Mix with   ½ cup honey or corn syrup
                         raisin/apricot mixture
Add   orange peel
                         1 cup chopped nutmeats
Mix thoroughly. Roll into small balls. These may be rolled in confec-
tioner's sugar. Makes about 36 balls.

MASHED FRUIT DESSERT

Mespel apples are fruits of the sapodilla tree. When this reddish fruit is
ripe, it feels soft. Cut it open and scoop out the creamy fruit inside.
Mix fruit with mashed banana. Grate on a little fresh nutmeg to go
with the apple's own cinnamon flavour. Chill and serve for dessert.

FRUIT SALAD IN GELATIN

My husband's mother made this every holiday, and served it as an
extra side dish. You can serve it as a dessert.

Prepare your favourite gelatin dessert, according to package
instructions. Drained juice from the pineapple may be used as part of
the liquid in preparing the gelatin. Chill until mixture is thick and
syrupy.
Mix in   1 cup chopped bananas
                         1 cup walnut halves
                         1 cup drained pineapple chunks
Chill until set.

For a festive touch, decorate top of dish, after gelatin has set, with more walnut halves, pineapple chunks, and banana slices dipped in pineapple juice to prevent discoloration.

STRAWBERRY BANANA FLAVOURED GELATIN

I can't really take credit for this recipe, but it would be remiss of me to leave it out.

Prepare a packet of commercial strawberry/banana flavoured gelatin according to package directions. Add one sliced or cubed banana before chilling. Serve plain or with whipped cream that has been slightly sweetened.

BANANA LIME CHIFFON

Chill a mixing bowl and beaters.

Also chill	6-oz can unsweetened evaporated milk
Mix together	1 pkg lime gelatin
	1 cup hot water
	4 pkgs Equal or other low calorie sweetener
	2 tbs lime juice
	2 tbs lemon juice

Chill until gelatin is like beaten egg white, but not totally set. When gelatin is syrupy, beat evaporated milk until stiff.

Dice	2 firm but ripe bananas

Fold beaten evaporated milk and diced bananas into gelatin mixture. Serve in dessert dishes, or half a canteloupe. Chill until firm, then garnish with half a slice of lime.

BANANA HONEY ICE-CREAM

Blend to a purée or mash well	1½ cups sliced banana
Beat in mixer on high speed until thick	3 egg yolks
Beat in	½ tsp grated lemon peel
	2 tbs lemon juice
	¼ tsp salt
Beat in puréed bananas.	
Add	¼ cup honey

Beat to soft peaks   1 cup whipping cream
Fold into banana mixture. Turn into 8×8×2 inch pan. Cover. Freeze until nearly solid. Break frozen mixture into chilled mixer bowl. Beat with electric mixer until smooth. Return to pan. Cover, freeze until firm. Makes 3 cups of ice-cream.

BANANA BOMBE

Whip	1½ pints heavy cream
Add	3 sliced bananas
	1 tsp vanilla
	¼ cup sugar
Spread firmly inside	
chilled bombe mould	1 quart chocolate ice-cream

Fill mould to the top with banana mixture. Cover with a piece of buttered waxed paper and then the mould cover. Freeze in refrigerator freezing compartment for 3–4 hours. Unmould on to a chilled serving dish. Serves 6.

FROZEN COMPOTE

Dissolve	1 cup sugar
in	1 pint boiling water
Add	¼ cup white Karo syrup
Meanwhile, shred	1 pineapple
Mash	1 banana
	1 cup strawberries
Add	juice of 1 lemon

Mix well. Pour syrup mixture on fruits, mix, then freeze for 30 minutes. Turn into a bowl and beat with electric mixer until smooth and creamy. Return to freezer and freeze until firm.

CAKES AND FROSTINGS

BANANA CAKE WITH CREAM CHEESE FROSTING

Preheat oven to 375°F. Grease and flour two 9-inch cake pans.

Cream together	2 sticks butter
	1 cup granulated sugar
Add, one at a time	2 eggs
Beat after each addition.	
Mix in	1 cup mashed ripe bananas
	1¾ cups flour
	½ tsp salt
	1 tsp baking soda
	5 tbs buttermilk
	1 tsp vanilla

Pour batter into prepared pans. Set on the middle rack in the oven and bake for 25–30 minutes at 375°F until a toothpick comes out clean. Cool in pans for 10 minutes. Unmould and cool on rack. When cooled, if desired, frost with Cream Cheese Frosting, below, then arrange banana slices, dipped in lemon juice, over frosted cake layers. Sides of cake may be covered with chopped nuts.

CREAM CHEESE FROSTING

Cream together	8 oz cream cheese
	6 tbs butter
	3 cups confectioner's sugar
	1 tsp vanilla
	juice of $\frac{1}{2}$ lemon

Use to frost a two-layer cake.

BANANA CREAM CAKE

Cream together	$\frac{1}{2}$ cup butter
	1 cup sugar
Add	3 well-beaten eggs
Separately, combine	1 tsp baking soda
	$\frac{1}{4}$ cup sour cream

Add to creamed mixture.

Add	1 cup mashed bananas
	1 tsp banana liqueur
Separately, mix together	$1\frac{1}{2}$ cups sifted flour
	1 tsp baking powder

Add dry ingredients to creamed mixture. Bake in buttered 8×8×2 inch pan at 375°F for 45 minutes, or until cake springs back when tested. Decorate with whipped cream and sliced bananas.

QUICK AND EASY BANANA CAKE

Beat	4 eggs
with	1 cup brown sugar
	1 medium mashed banana (about $\frac{1}{2}$ cup)
Add	2 cups prepared biscuit mix
	1 cup pecans
	1 cup coconut

Pour into greased 9×13 inch pan. Bake for 30–40 minutes at 350°F. Cake is done when it springs back at the touch.

MIXED FRUIT CAKE

Combine	2 cups sifted flour
	3 tsp baking powder
Separately, combine	$\frac{3}{4}$ cup chopped candied fruit
	$\frac{1}{2}$ cup walnuts, chopped
	$\frac{1}{2}$ cup of flour mixture

Cream	$\frac{1}{4}$ cup shortening
	$\frac{1}{2}$ cup butter
	1 cup sugar
Add	2 eggs
Beat well.	
Combine	1 cup mashed bananas
	1 tbs lemon juice

Blend bananas into creamed mixture. Add remaining flour mixture. Blend well. Fold in floured fruit and nuts. Bake in $9 \times 5 \times 3$ inch pan at 350°F for 60–70 minutes.

BANANA CRISP (1)

Cut	1 cube butter ($\frac{1}{4}$ lb)
into	1 pkg yellow cake mix

Mixture should resemble crumbs.

In a saucepan, mix	
together	1 cup orange juice
	1 tsp cornstarch

Heat together until thick.

Slice in	4 medium bananas

Pour bananas and sauce into a buttered $8 \times 8 \times 2$ inch baking pan. Top with crumb mixture. Bake at 375°F for 30–35 minutes, or until crumb topping is crisp and brown. Serve plain, or with ice-cream or whipped cream.

BANANA CRISP (2)

In a well-buttered	
baking dish, layer	4 cups sliced bananas
with mixture of	1 tsp cinnamon
	1 tsp salt
	$\frac{1}{4}$ cup water

Meanwhile, in a	
separate bowl, mix	
together	$\frac{3}{4}$ cup flour
	1 cup brown sugar
	$\frac{1}{3}$ cup soft butter

Pour this mixture over bananas. Bake at 350°F for about 40 minutes, or until crisp and brown.

BANANA SPICE CAKE

Sift together	$2\frac{1}{2}$ cups flour
	$1\frac{1}{2}$ cups sugar
	$2\frac{1}{2}$ tsp baking powder
	$\frac{1}{2}$ tsp soda
	1 tsp cinnamon
	$\frac{1}{2}$ tsp cloves
	1 tsp freshly grated nutmeg
Add	1 cube butter ($\frac{1}{4}$ lb) (softened)
	1 cup mashed banana
	3 eggs
	$\frac{1}{2}$ cup buttermilk
	$\frac{1}{2}$ cup dark Karo syrup

Mix with electric mixer until ingredients are well blended. Pour into two 9-inch round pans which have been greased and floured. Bake at 350°F for 30–35 minutes, or until cake springs back when touched. Sprinkle lightly with powdered sugar.

BANANA UPSIDE DOWN CAKE

In a 9×9×2 inch cake pan, melt	3 tbs butter
Sprinkle evenly with	1 cup brown sugar (or less)
	1 tsp cinnamon
	$\frac{1}{4}$ cup orange juice

Heat mixture until syrup is formed and is very hot.

Over the syrup mixture, arrange	3 sliced bananas
	broken walnut pieces
Meanwhile, beat until light and thick	2 eggs
Add	$\frac{3}{4}$ cup sugar
Sift together	1 cup flour
	1 tsp baking powder

Fold flour into egg and sugar mixture.

Add	1 tsp vanilla
	$\frac{1}{2}$ cup hot milk
	2 tbs oil or melted butter

Blend thoroughly, then pour batter over hot fruit in cake tin. Bake for 30–35 minutes in 375°F oven. Let stand 5 minutes, then turn out on to serving plate. May be served warm or cold. Especially good when served warm and topped with scoops of vanilla ice-cream.

FROSTED BANANA NUT CAKE

Mix together	2 cups baking mix
	$\frac{1}{2}$ cup sugar
	$\frac{1}{2}$ cup mashed bananas
	$\frac{1}{4}$ cup buttermilk
	2 tbs butter
	2 eggs
	$\frac{1}{2}$ cup chopped nuts

Pour into greased and floured 8×8×2 inch pan. Bake at 350°F for about 25 minutes, or until cake springs back when touched with the fingers.

BROWNED BUTTER FROSTING

Brown in heavy pan	
over low heat	3 tbs butter
Add	2 cups powdered sugar
	1 tsp vanilla

Mix well. Then add milk or water, a little at a time: about 4–5 tbs should give you a frosting of smooth consistency. Spread over cake.

BANANA WALNUT SNACKING CAKE

Heat oven to 350°F.

Mix	$1\frac{1}{4}$ cups flour
with	$\frac{3}{4}$ cup sugar
	$\frac{3}{4}$ tsp baking powder
	$\frac{3}{4}$ tsp baking soda
	$\frac{1}{2}$ tsp salt
	$\frac{1}{3}$ cup chopped walnuts
	$\frac{1}{2}$ cup mashed banana (about 1 medium)
Pour on	$\frac{1}{2}$ cup buttermilk
	$\frac{1}{3}$ cup vegetable oil
Break in	1 egg

Mix thoroughly with a fork for 1–2 minutes, or until no dry ingredients remain. Place in an ungreased square baking pan (9×9×2 inches). Bake until wooden pick inserted in centre comes out clean (30–35 minutes). Cool.

BANANA NUT CAKE

Crush into a mixing cup	2 very ripe bananas
Add	enough oil to make $\frac{2}{3}$ cup

If bananas exceed $\frac{2}{3}$ cup do not add any oil and decrease wine (see below) to make a total liquid of $1\frac{1}{3}$ cups.

Add	$\frac{2}{3}$ cup cream sherry or rum
	4 eggs
	1 pkg banana cake mix
	1 pkg banana instant pudding mix
	$\frac{3}{4}$ cup chopped walnuts

Mix well, then beat with electric mixer until smooth and creamy. Bake in two loaf pans, greased and floured, at 375°F for 45 minutes, or until cake springs back at the touch.

If you don't have very ripe bananas, use $\frac{2}{3}$ cup oil. The flavour will still be banana and, unless you tell them, your guests will never know that the cake contains absolutely no bananas.

CHOCOLATE ALMOND BANANA CAKE

Mix together	2 ripe bananas, mashed
	$\frac{1}{2}$ cup rum
	4 eggs
	1 pkg yellow cake mix
	1 pkg chocolate-flavour instant pudding

Bake in the same way as Banana Nut Cake, above.

ALMOND MOCHA BANANA CAKE

Use the Chocolate Almond Banana Cake recipe above.

Add	1 tbs instant coffee
	4-oz pkg chopped almonds

Bake in the same way as Banana Nut Cake, above.

BANANA SHORTCAKE

Mix together	1 cup biscuit mix
	$\frac{1}{2}$ cup milk
	$\frac{1}{4}$ cup melted butter
	2 tbs sugar

Beat well, turn on to floured board and knead well. Roll dough to $\frac{1}{2}$-inch thickness. Cut with floured 3-inch cutter. Bake at 400°F on an ungreased baking sheet for about 10 minutes, or until nicely browned.

To prepare banana filling:

Dice	2 cups bananas
Add	2 tbs lemon juice
	2 tbs sugar

Mix well. To assemble: split shortcakes crosswise while warm; spread with butter; spoon on sweetened fruit; top with second layer, then more fruit. Serve with cream: sweetened whipped cream, or commercial sour cream.

ORANGE BANANA SHORTCAKE

Sift together in bowl	2 cups flour
	2 pkgs Equal or other low calorie sweetener
	1 tbs baking powder
Cut in	$\frac{1}{2}$ cup butter

Continue until mixture is like coarse meal.

Pour on	$\frac{1}{2}$ cup evaporated milk

Stir with a fork until dough makes a ball. Put dough on floured surface and knead lightly. When dough is smooth, divide in half. Gently roll each part into a round about half an inch thick and put one in an 8-inch round cake pan. Brush with melted butter and top with other round. Brush top of that with more melted butter. Bake at 400°F for 18–20 minutes, or until browned.

To assemble: cut shortcake into two layers. Place one layer on a plate and cover with half a quantity of Banana Orange Topping (see below). Top with second cake layer. Cover that with remaining topping and, if desired, sweetened, whipped cream.

BANANA ORANGE TOPPING

Peel and section	2 oranges
	2 medium, ripe bananas
Mix fruit together and add	$\frac{1}{2}$ cup orange juice
	2 pkgs Equal or other low calorie sweetener

LOW CALORIE BANANA CAKELETS

Grease and flour 12 muffin cups, or line baking cups with paper.

Sift together	2 cups flour
	2 tsp baking powder
	$\frac{1}{2}$ tsp soda
	$\frac{1}{2}$ tsp freshly grated nutmeg
Separately, combine	1 lightly beaten egg
	1 cup mashed ripe banana

$\frac{1}{3}$ cup skimmed milk
$\frac{1}{3}$ cup vegetable oil
2 pkgs Equal or other low calorie
    sweetener

Add wet ingredients to dry, mixing to moisten throughout. Fill baking cups just over half full. Bake at 375°F for 15–20 minutes until golden-brown and cakes spring back when touched.

Cakes may be topped with Banana Orange Topping (see Orange Banana Shortcake*) or Low Calorie Banana Orange Topping*.

SOUR CREAM BANANA BARS

Heat oven to 375°F. Grease and flour jelly-roll pan, $15\frac{1}{2} \times 10\frac{1}{2} \times 1$ inches.

Mix together	$1\frac{1}{2}$ cups sugar
	1 cup dairy sour cream
	$\frac{1}{2}$ cup softened butter or margarine
	2 eggs

Mix on low speed for one minute, scraping bowl occasionally.

| *Beat in* | $1\frac{1}{2}$ cups mashed bananas |
| | 2 tsp vanilla |

Mix on low speed for 30 seconds.

Beat in and mix well	2 cups all-purpose flour
	1 tsp salt
	1 tsp baking soda
Stir in	$\frac{1}{2}$ cup chopped nuts

Spread dough in pan. Bake until lightly browned for 20–25 minutes. Cool. Cut into bars. Frost with Browned Butter Frosting (see Frosted Banana Nut Cake*).

BANANA DREAM BARS

| *Cut* | $\frac{1}{2}$ cup butter |
| *into* | 1 cup sifted flour |

Press mixture into bottom of an ungreased 11×7 inch pan. Bake in moderate 350°F oven for 15–18 minutes until just set but not brown.

Combine	2 beaten eggs
	$\frac{1}{2}$ cup packed brown sugar
	$\frac{3}{4}$ cup coconut, chopped
	$\frac{1}{2}$ tsp baking powder
	$\frac{1}{4}$ tsp salt
	$\frac{1}{2}$ tsp vanilla

Spread over partially-baked dough. Bake at 350°F for 18–22 minutes. Frost immediately (see below). Cool for 15 minutes, cut into bars.

BANANA FROSTING (1)

Combine	1 cup sifted confectioner's sugar
	2 tbs mashed banana
	2 tbs lemon juice

Mix until smooth, spreading consistency is reached, adjusting amount of lemon juice if necessary.

SPICY BANANA BARS

Cream	1 mashed banana
with	1 cup shortening
Add	1 egg

Beat one minute.

Add	$\frac{3}{4}$ cup sugar
	$\frac{1}{2}$ tsp baking powder
	$\frac{1}{4}$ tsp soda
	$1\frac{1}{2}$ cups flour
	$\frac{3}{4}$ tsp cinnamon
	$\frac{1}{4}$ tsp nutmeg
	$\frac{1}{4}$ cup buttermilk
Mix well, then add	$\frac{1}{3}$ cup chopped pecans

Fold in. Bake in 9×13 inch pan at 350°F for 20 minutes. When cool, frost (see below).

BANANA FROSTING (2)

Cream	1 tbs butter
with	1 cup powdered sugar
Add	$1\frac{1}{2}$ tbs mashed banana
	$\frac{1}{2}$ tsp lemon juice

Blend well.

See also Banana Daiquiri Pie* filling and Cream Cheese Frosting* for use as cake toppings or fillings. Two more ideas for toppings are as follows.

BANANA ICING

| *Mash* | $\frac{1}{2}$ cup ripe bananas |
| *Stir in* | 2 cups confectioner's sugar |

Beat in   ⅛ tsp salt
                                 1 tsp vanilla
                                 1 tsp lemon juice
Add more sugar if needed to achieve consistency of icing wanted.

LOW CALORIE BANANA ORANGE TOPPING

Mix together   ½ cup orange juice
                                 1½ tsp cornstarch
Add   1 beaten egg
Cook over medium heat, stirring constantly, until mixture boils.
Remove from heat.
Stir in   ½ cup mashed banana
                                 1 pkg Equal or other low calorie
                                 sweetener
Chill bowl, beaters, and   ⅓ cup evaporated milk
Whip with   2 tbs fresh lemon juice
When stiff, fold in orange/banana mixture. Serve immediately as
topping for cakes, desserts or salads.

BREADS AND COOKIES

CARIBBEAN BANANA FRUIT BREAD

Preheat oven to 350°F.

Mix together to a
crumb-like texture

$1\frac{3}{4}$ cups flour
$\frac{2}{3}$ cup sugar
2 tsp baking powder
$\frac{1}{2}$ tsp salt
$\frac{1}{8}$ tsp baking soda
$\frac{1}{3}$ cup butter or margarine

Mash   3 very ripe bananas

Add to other ingredients and blend well.

Mix in

1 jigger banana liqueur
2 eggs
$\frac{1}{2}$ cup chopped walnuts or pecans
$\frac{1}{8}$ cup candied orange peel
$\frac{1}{2}$ cup chopped cherries
$\frac{1}{4}$ cup chopped candied pineapple
$\frac{1}{8}$ cup chopped citron
$\frac{1}{4}$ cup raisins

Blend well. Pour into 9×5 inch baking pan and bake for 1¼ hours. Let cool in pan for 1 hour. Take out and leave until completely cold. Wrap in foil and keep for 24 hours before serving.

BANANA BREAD
(a gift from the tropics)

Cream together	⅓ cup shortening
	¾ cup sugar
	2 bananas, sliced
Add	1 egg

Beat mixture until well blended.

Separately, combine	2 cups sifted flour
	1 tsp baking powder
	½ tsp soda
	1 tsp salt
	¾ cup buttermilk

Gently stir dry ingredients into wet mixture. Mix well and turn into loaf pan greased with shortening. Bake at 350°F for about an hour.

BANANA NUT LOAF
Add ½ cup chopped nuts before pouring mixture above into loaf pan

PRUNE OR APRICOT LOAF
Add to mixture above ¾ cup dried prunes or apricots, cooked, drained and mashed, and ¾ cup juice from the fruit instead of buttermilk. Stir in also the grated rind of a lemon.

BANANA MUFFINS

Mix together well	2 cups baking mix
	2 tbs sugar
	¾ cup milk
	1 beaten egg
Fold in	1 cup chopped banana
For richer muffins, add	2 tbs more sugar
	2 tbs soft shortening

Fill greased medium-sized muffin cups two-thirds full. Bake for 15 minutes at 400°F. Makes 12 muffins.

BANANA SURPRISE FILLED MUFFINS

Combine
$1\frac{3}{4}$ cups flour
$\frac{1}{3}$ cup sugar
2 tsp baking powder
$\frac{3}{4}$ tsp salt
$\frac{1}{4}$ tsp soda

Mix well. Make a well in centre of mixture.

Add
1 egg, well beaten
$\frac{1}{3}$ cup vegetable oil
1 cup mashed ripe banana

Stir until just moistened. Spoon into greased muffin pans. Fill only one-third full. Spoon 1 tsp jelly on to centre of each muffin. Spoon remaining batter over jelly, filling each cup two-thirds full. Bake for 15 minutes at 400°F.

BANANA BRAN MUFFINS

Sift together
1 cup flour
$\frac{1}{2}$ tsp soda
$\frac{1}{4}$ cup sugar

Add
1 cup bran cereal

Mix well.

Separately, combine
1 well-beaten egg
2 tbs buttermilk or sour milk
2 tbs oil
2 cups thinly sliced bananas

Add dry ingredients and mix well. Turn into well-greased muffin tins. Bake at 375°F for 35 minutes. Makes 6 large muffins. Leftovers, if there are any, may be split and toasted.

BANANA SURPRISE MERINGUE MUFFINS

In a small bowl, mix
$\frac{1}{4}$ cup flour
$\frac{1}{2}$ cup wholewheat flour
2 tbs sugar
1 tsp baking powder
$\frac{1}{8}$ tsp baking soda

Make a well in centre.

Combine
1 egg yolk
$\frac{1}{2}$ cup milk
2 tbs butter, melted

Add all at once to centre of dry ingredients. Stir until just moistened. Batter will be lumpy, but do not worry.

Fold in   1 small banana, finely chopped

                            2 tbs chopped pecans

Spoon into greased and floured 2¾-inch muffin cups, filling each only three-quarters full. Bake at 400°F for about 10 minutes. Remove from oven.

Meanwhile, beat to soft
peaks   1 egg white

Gradually add   3 tbs sugar

Beat to stiff peaks. Spread meringue evenly over each muffin, and, if desired, top with ½ tsp jelly or jam. Return to 400°F oven for 10–15 minutes more or until browned and muffins are done when tested with toothpick. Serve warm. Makes 6 muffins.

See also Heavenly Triple Banana Breakfast Muffins*.

WHOLEWHEAT BANANA BISCUITS

Mix together   2 cups wholewheat flour

                            ¼ cup soy flour

                            3 tsp baking powder

                            ½ tsp baking soda

                            1 tsp sugar

                            1 tsp salt

Cut in   ½ cup softened butter

Work until mixture resembles cornmeal.

Add   ½ cup dairy sour cream

                            ½ cup (about 1 medium) mashed ripe
                            banana

Then add   enough milk to hold mixture together
                            (less than ¼ cup)

Stir with fork only until dry ingredients are moistened. Turn out on lightly floured board and knead 10 turns. Roll gently to ½-inch thickness and cut into rounds with 2-inch cutter. Put on ungreased baking sheet, prick with fork and bake in preheated 450°F oven for 10 minutes, or until well browned. Serve at once with butter and jam, if desired. Makes about 20 biscuits.

BANANA ROCKS

These are thick, soft, oatmeal cookies containing raisins, dates, prunes, nuts and banana.

Sift together	1½ cups flour
	½ tsp baking soda
	1 tsp cinnamon
	¼ tsp nutmeg
	¼ tsp ginger
Place in a mixing bowl	¾ cup raisins
	¾ cup pitted dates, quartered
	¾ cup uncooked, pitted prunes, quartered

Add a large spoonful of the sifted, dry ingredients and, with your fingers, toss the fruit until all pieces are coated and separated.

Add	1½ cups walnut pieces

Toss again.

Mash	bananas to make 1 cup
Beat in	1 egg
Cream	4 oz (1 stick) butter
with	1 cup dark-brown sugar, firmly packed

Add banana/egg mixture to butter and sugar. Blend until smooth.

Add	grated rind of 2 lemons
	fruit/nut mixture
Then beat in	1½ cups old-fashioned oatmeal
and	dry ingredients

Using a heaped teaspoon of dough for each cookie, drop spoonfuls 2 inches apart on foil-lined cookie sheet. Pile up dough and do not flatten. Bake for 15–16 minutes at 400°F. If you have 2 pans in oven at the same time, reverse pans to bake evenly. Cookies are done when they spring back when touched with fingertip. Do not overbake. They should remain soft.

While cookies are baking prepare glaze:

Combine	3 tbs soft butter
	1½ cups confectioner's sugar
	3 tbs milk

Slide foil and cookies off cookie sheet on to cooling rack. Immediately, while cookies are very hot, brush on glaze. Work quickly so the heat of the cookie will melt the glaze and let it run down the sides unevenly. Remove foil to allow glaze to dry completely.

BANANA OATMEAL COOKIES

Sift	1½ cups flour
with	½ tsp soda
	½ tsp nutmeg

	$\frac{1}{2}$ tsp cinnamon
Beat until creamy	$\frac{3}{4}$ cup shortening
Add and beat in	1 cup sugar
Add and beat well	1 egg
Mix in	1 cup mashed banana (2–3 bananas)
	$1\frac{1}{2}$ cups regular oatmeal
	$\frac{1}{2}$ cup chopped nuts
	flour mixture

Drop teaspoonfuls of mixture about 2 inches apart on to foil-lined baking sheet. Bake at 400°F for about 12 minutes. Remove from baking pan to wire rack to cool.

CHOCOLATE BANANA COOKIES

Adjust two racks to divide oven into thirds, then preheat oven to 400°F. Line cookie sheets with foil.

Melt in double boiler	6 oz chocolate chips

Set aside to cool.

Mix together	$2\frac{1}{2}$ cups flour, sifted
	2 tsp baking powder
	$\frac{1}{4}$ tsp baking soda
	1 cup mashed banana
	4 oz butter
	1 tsp vanilla
	$\frac{1}{4}$ cup banana liqueur
	1 cup granulated sugar
	2 eggs

When thoroughly mixed, pour in melted chocolate. Blend.

Add	$\frac{1}{2}$ cup chopped walnuts

With heaped teaspoonfuls (make large cookies), make mounds 2 inches apart on the foil-lined cookie sheets. Bake for 10–12 minutes, reversing pans after half the baking time for even cooking. Cookies are done when centre springs back when touched. Slide foil and cookies off baking sheets. Let stand a moment, then gently transfer cookies to racks to cool. Makes about 50 cookies.

DRINKS

BANANA MARGUERITA

For those who think of the Marguerita as a mixture of tequila and orange liqueur, take a leaf from the tropical book: try adding some strawberries — *voilà*, Strawberry Marguerita; or bananas, and you have Banana Marguerita.

Mix together	2 parts tequila
	1 part Triple Sec
	1 part lime juice
Drop in	½ ripe banana, peeled

Blend to mix, then add crushed ice until it comes above liquid in blender. Blend on high until the ice is well mixed in. Use a shaker if you have no blender, but crack the ice finer than for a blender. Rub rim of glass with a cut lime, pour in Marguerita and savour. Some call this a Banana Rita, but to us it is just a Marguerita with half a banana added.

FRUIT CUP

A mixed fruit cup is just that — a mixture of fruits. It can be all fresh, part fresh and part tinned, or all tinned. Hopefully, you will have at least one fresh fruit in yours, as it makes for a better cup. One fresh, crisp, chopped apple added to a can of mixed fruit can make you believe the whole serving is fresh.

Cut any fresh fruit into bite-sized pieces — not too small. Mix together and serve either in their own juice, or add $\frac{1}{4}$ cup of orange, grapefruit, pineapple, or apple juice per serving.
Alternatively: mix a tin of fruits for salad with a sliced banana, cut-up apple or orange. This is a great way to use up that one leftover slice of melon or one remaining grapefruit or banana. For something special, add a tablespoon of orange liqueur to each serving.

BANANA MILK SHAKE

Combine   2 cups cold milk
                         2 medium bananas
Beat with rotary beater or mix in blender until frothy.
Add   2–4 scoops vanilla ice-cream
Beat until well blended. Serve.

BANANA CHOCOLATE MILK SHAKE
Make as for Banana Milk Shake, but add $\frac{1}{4}$ cup chocolate syrup to the first stage.
See also Banana Breakfast Shake*.

BANANA SUPERSHAKE

In blender, mix   2 ripe bananas, sliced
                         $\frac{1}{2}$ cup fresh lemon juice
                         1 can sweetened condensed milk
Blend well, then gradually add, with blender running, 3 cups crushed ice and mix until sound changes on blender, or until there is no sign of circular motion on top of mixture. Serve with a straw and a spoon because the shake will be very thick.
If desired, other fruits can be mixed with the bananas, such as strawberries, peeled and sectioned oranges, blackberries, etc.

BANANA CHOCOLATE FLOAT

Dice and put in a glass   1 banana

Add   1 tbs chocolate syrup

$\frac{1}{2}$ tsp vanilla

$\frac{1}{4}$ tsp almond essence

Mix with spoon.
Using electric mixer,
beat until just smooth   2 scoops vanilla ice-cream
Add and beat, just until
mixed   1 cup cold milk

Pour over banana mixture in glass. Stir lightly with spoon —
delicious!

ODDS AND ENDS

In our attempts to come up with different ways of using the banana, we have almost forgotten the easiest way of all — just peel it and eat it! Rich in vitamins A and C, low in fat, easily digested when ripe, the banana is a highly valued food source. Recently, it has been adopted by sportsmen into their diet as a prevention against muscular cramp. Of course, one of the banana's most common uses is as a **baby food**: just mash a ripe, peeled banana with a fork and you are ready to feed your baby one of the first foods many doctors recommend. What could be easier or more natural?

In fact, children of all ages adore bananas. Why not try mixing fillings for two perennial sandwich favourites — banana and peanut butter? Here are a few more recipes which are popular with youngsters.

FROZEN CHOCOLATE BANANA ON A STICK

Peel firm, ripe bananas. Carefully insert a popsicle stick in one end of each banana. Freeze on a cookie sheet until solid. Melt chocolate chips, about 2 oz per banana. Carefully dip each frozen banana into melted chocolate until it is evenly coated. Return to freezer to harden chocolate.

ORANGE BANANA POPS

Combine	3 medium bananas, mashed (about 2 cups)
	1 cup orange juice
	2 tbs sugar
	about $\frac{1}{4}$ cup water
	1 tsp lime juice

Mix well. Pour into 6 (5 oz) plastic cups. Partially freeze. Insert wooden stick in each. Freeze completely. When ready to eat, let stand at room temperature for 5 minutes. Remove cups and enjoy.

BANANA FUDGE

Mix together	2 cups white sugar
	$\frac{1}{3}$ cup water
	$\frac{1}{3}$ cup milk
	2 tbs butter
	2 mashed bananas
	2 tbs corn syrup

Bring to a soft boil stage. Pour mixture into a buttered, shallow pan. Mark into squares while warm. Then leave until quite cold.

BANANA JAM (1)

Cut into $\frac{1}{2}$-inch slices	7 lbs very ripe bananas
Mix together with	3 cups sugar
	1 cup orange juice
	$\frac{3}{4}$ cup lemon juice

Bring mixture to a boil in a large pan. Boil rapidly and stir constantly for about 10 minutes. Reduce heat and simmer, stirring frequently until moderately thick, about 15 minutes. Pour into clean, warm jars. Cover and seal while hot. Makes 2 quarts of banana jam.

BANANA JAM (2)

Peel and slice	6 ripe bananas
Grate on	rind of 4 limes
Squeeze on	juice of same 4 limes
Add	1 lb white sugar

Heat slowly to boiling. Boil, stirring constantly until set. Bottle, cover and seal tops.

SEYCHELLES BANAE EN FRITES

Cut green bananas or plantains into thin slices. Fry in deep fat. Drain. Salt to taste. Serve as a snack, or with drinks.

HINTS

SECTIONING BANANAS

For something different, instead of slicing bananas lengthwise, you can break them into three natural sections. To start, peel the fruit, then, using your knife, very carefully slit the end of the banana. Now, slip one finger into the opening and carefully break the fruit into sections. It will naturally divide into three parts with no knife marks. (See Banana Lumpia*.)

STORING BANANAS

If bananas are ripe, do not refrigerate or the skin will become discoloured. If, however, you are not ready to use them, peel bananas and place the fruit in a plastic bag. Squeeze, or use a straw to remove air. Seal the bag. Freeze. When you are ready to use the bananas in cooking or any recipe that calls for mashed banana, defrost in the bag and measure out the quantity you need for your recipe. Proceed as if you were using fresh, mashed, ripe banana.

Alternatively, cut that ripe banana into bite-sized cubes. Freeze on a cookie sheet and when fully frozen, store in the freezer in a plastic bag. When you feel the need for something sweet, pop one of these refreshing morsels in your mouth. If a whole banana contains 100 calories, a $\frac{1}{2}$-inch slice will contain very few calories.

EVERYDAY USE

Let underripe bananas ripen at room temperature. Ripe ones should have a yellow skin flecked with brown. When buying bananas, avoid fruit with soft, dark tips and discoloured skin. Use slightly underripe bananas in cooking, unless you are mashing them for use in bread or cookies.

Do not serve bananas as part of your fruit bowl unless they have reached the right stage of ripeness, which is the only way to appreciate this delicious fruit.

Once a banana has been peeled, sprinkle it with lemon juice as the flesh turns brown when exposed to the air. Fruit salad which contains banana can also be covered with orange or pineapple juice and then drained just before serving — the citrus juice will enhance the flavour of the salad and keep the bananas from discolouring.

PLANTAIN

These are 9–12 inches long. They resemble bananas but they must be cooked. Otherwise, they are very hard, their flavour is starchy and not very appetising. When cooked, they are more suitable for savoury dishes as they are not really sweet. Be careful not to overcook them as this might make them bitter-tasting. Green plantains must be peeled with a knife, for they are reluctant to part with their skins. Be careful to remove all the fibrous strings before cooking, as these will darken and make the end result less palatable.

They can be successfully added to omelettes, soups or stews. Dice finely and add towards the end of the cooking process. When sautéing, slice into circular or oval shapes and cook slowly until tender. Similarly, when boiling, as for Tropical Salad*, boil until tender. Test with a fork. Do not overcook. They can be boiled in rapidly boiling water for about 30 minutes, seasoned with butter, salt and pepper, and served as a vegetable, much like potato or sweet potato. Use them as a substitute for potatoes in a potato salad — watch for your guests' surprise!

MEASUREMENTS AND CONVERSION TABLES

STANDARD MEASURES

1 teaspoon	=	$\frac{1}{6}$ fluid ounce
1 tablespoon	=	$\frac{1}{2}$ fluid ounce
1 cup	=	8 fluid ounces

MEASUREMENT EQUIVALENTS

1 tablespoon	=	3 tsp
1 cup	=	16 tablespoons
$\frac{1}{4}$ cup	=	4 tablespoons
$\frac{3}{8}$ cup	=	6 tablespoons
$\frac{5}{8}$ cup	=	$\frac{1}{2}$ cup + 2 tablespoons
$\frac{7}{8}$ cup	=	$\frac{3}{4}$ cup + 2 tablespoons

METRIC CONVERSIONS
(These are approximate conversions based on 25 ml or 25 g units.)

Liquids		Solids	
1 fl oz	25 ml	1 oz	25 g
2 fl oz	50 ml	2 oz	50 g
3 fl oz	75 ml	3 oz	75 g
4 fl oz	100 ml	4 oz	100 g
5 fl oz	150 ml	5 oz	150 g
6 fl oz	175 ml	6 oz	175 g
7 fl oz	200 ml	7 oz	200 g
8 fl oz	225 ml	8 oz ($\frac{1}{2}$ lb)	225 g
9 fl oz	250 ml	9 oz	250 g
10 fl oz	275 ml	10 oz	275 g
11 fl oz	300 ml	11 oz	300 g
12 fl oz	350 ml	12 oz	350 g
13 fl oz	375 ml	13 oz	375 g
14 fl oz	400 ml	14 oz	400 g
15 fl oz	425 ml	15 oz	425 g
16 fl oz	450 ml	16 oz (1 lb)	450 g
17 fl oz	475 ml	17 oz	475 g
18 fl oz	500 ml	18 oz	500 g
19 fl oz	550 ml	19 oz	550 g
20 fl oz	575 ml	20 oz	575 g
30 fl oz	850 ml	24 oz	700 g
35 fl oz	1000 ml	36 oz	900 g

TEMPERATURES

Farenheit (F)		Celcius (C)
0°		–17°
32°	water freezes	0°
115°	water simmers	46°
130°	water scalds	54°
212°	water boils	100°
250°–275°	very low oven	121°–133°
300°–325°	low oven	149°–163°
350°–375°	moderate oven	177°–190°
400°–425°	hot oven	204°–218°
450°–525°	very hot oven	232°–274°

In this book, temperatures, are in °F.

TRANSLATIONS

English	American
1 pint = 20 fl oz	1 pint = 16 fl oz
Quart	32 fl oz
Gil	5 fl oz
4 oz butter	1 stick butter
Castor sugar	Nearest equivalent is super fine
Cornflour	Cornstarch
Heavy or double cream	Whipping cream
Tin	Can

In this book, 1 pint = 16 fl oz; tablespoon measurements are American Standard, therefore smaller than British Standard.

INDEX